Children

CHOICES

GUIDES FOR TODAY'S WOMAN

Children

Laura Lein
and
Lydia O'Donnell

The Westminster Press
Philadelphia

The excerpt in Chapter 2 from "Maternity Costs:
Parenthood and Career Overtax Some Women Despite Best Intentions," by Barbara Toman, is re-
printed by permission of *The Wall Street Journal* ©
Dow Jones & Company, Inc. 1983. All Rights Re-
served.

Book design by Alice Derr

First edition

Published by The Westminster Press®
Philadelphia, Pennsylvania

PRINTED IN THE UNITED STATES OF AMERICA
9 8 7 6 5 4 3 2 1

Library of Congress Cataloging in Publication Data

Lein, Laura, 1947–
  Children.

  (Choices ; 9)
  Bibliography: p.
  1. Parenting. 2. Parents—Attitudes. 3. Parents—
Psychology. 4. Parent and child. I. O'Donnell, Lydia,
1949–   . II. Title. III. Series.
HQ755.8.L44   1984   649'.1   84-7543
ISBN 0-664-24550-1 (pbk.)

To
Anna, Blake, and Rebecca
who have shown us the pleasures of parenting

.

CONTENTS

PUBLISHER'S ACKNOWLEDGMENT

The publisher gratefully acknowledges the advice of several distinguished scholars in planning this series. Virginia Mollenkott, Arlene Swidler, Phyllis Trible, and Ann Ulanov helped shape the goals of the series, identify vital topics, and locate knowledgeable authors. Views expressed in the books, of course, are those of the individual writers and not of the advisers.

CHAPTER 1

Responsibility for Children: A Stage in Adult Lives

The decision whether or not to have children is one of the most profound and consequential choices most of us ever face. Since we live in an age of choice, each of us must consider whether we are ready, willing, and able to take on the responsibilities of parenting, to commit ourselves to raising the next generation. Even amid the most pleasant thoughts of cuddly infants and appealing toddlers, it is the rare person who does not experience some doubt and apprehension at the prospect of parenthood. How will having a child change my life? How will it affect my marriage? Will I like being a parent? Will I be good at it? In what ways will a child tie me down? Is it worth having children anymore? And, ultimately, is it possible to raise a child successfully in our confusing, rapidly changing, and often dangerous world?

These are the types of questions we address in the following pages. We don't chart the physical and emotional stages of pregnancy, nor do we list 101 ways to deal with a colicky baby or a rebellious teenager. There are many other books available today that provide this type of advice. Rather, we take a broader view and examine how becoming a parent and taking on the responsibility of child rearing shapes the lives of contemporary mothers and fathers.

First, we consider why men and women, given more freedom and a greater range of opportunities and choices than either their parents or their grandparents had before them, continue to want children. While there have been numerous accounts recently of couples who have decided to remain childless, the vast majority of adults today become parents, just like those of earlier generations. More men and women may be choosing to delay parenthood until they reach their late twenties and even early thirties, but eventually they become parents nonetheless. One has only to witness the determination and anguish of couples who have fertility problems to realize how strong the desire to become a parent can be. As researchers who have asked young adults about their future plans and aspirations have discovered, most of us expect to become parents at some point in our lives; parenthood is still looked upon as a normal stage of the life course. In the following, we explore the reasons why men and women want children and the ways in which children enrich the lives of their parents.

In addition to looking at the positive aspects and potential rewards of child rearing, however, we also provide a realistic look at how the responsibilities of child rearing shape and at times constrain the lives of mothers and fathers. In our society, as in most others around the world, parenthood continues to affect the lives of men and women in different ways. In preparing for a life with children, it is helpful to understand

and acknowledge these differences. We therefore address how parenthood fits into the lives of men and women and how it changes the activities and commitments of members of each sex. Because in most families women continue to be responsible for the majority of child care, we pay particular attention to how motherhood fits into a woman's life, how it shapes the way she feels about her career potential and her paid work, and how it affects her relationships with her husband, her own parents, her friends and neighbors, and the wider community.

To have children is to make a commitment—to them, to ourselves, and to the future. Many people have labeled those of us currently in our child-rearing years as a selfish, narcissistic generation, one that has been unsuccessful at making even the most basic of personal commitments. We have been criticized for thinking only of ourselves, for pursuing our own personal advancement to the exclusion of the needs of others. Critics cite the high proportion of marriages that fail, the number of children who are left to be raised by one parent, the decline of traditional family, religious, and community values. Yet despite the difficulties and harsh realities of modern life, most of us make a commitment to having and raising children. What such a commitment entails is the subject of this book.

In the following chapters, we draw on many different studies of the parenting experience. We incorporate research that has been conducted over the past twenty years by scholars from a variety of disciplines, including the work of sociologists, economists, anthropologists, and psychologists. In addition, we rely on data we have gathered personally over the past five years as part of our own investigation of the changing roles of women and contemporary American family life. Through this work we have interviewed approximately two hundred mothers, as well as many of their husbands. These interviews have given us insights into what it means to be a parent today; whenever possible, we use quotations and examples from this research to illustrate our points.

WHY HAVE CHILDREN? THE ECONOMIC COSTS AND PERSONAL BENEFITS OF CHILD REARING

For several decades, economists have tried to construct a model that would explain, in dollars and cents, why anyone would choose to have children. Until relatively recent times, youngsters were most often viewed as financial assets to their families. On farms even young boys and girls were expected to provide a much-needed share of the physical labor. In cities older children typically held paid jobs that helped put food on the table. In addition, each member of the family, young and old, was expected to contribute to domestic chores. While men and women probably never have had children in order actually to make money, it is easy to see how children contributed to the economic maintenance of their households. Indeed, large families were often seen as an economic plus rather than as a burden.

Because of changes in the nature of work in an industrialized society and also protective legislation such as the child labor laws, however, the work of children has become of much less economic importance. These days, in most cases, children's financial contributions to family life are considered negligible by their parents. The scales have actually turned. The financial benefits of having children are vastly outweighed by the financial burdens of child rearing. The estimated average cost of raising a child, including the expense of a college education, now approaches $200,000. In 1970, when many of those currently having children were themselves going to college, the average cost of room, board, and tuition at a private college for four years was $12,000. Increasing much faster than inflation or salaries, the same education today would cost four times this amount. How, parents ask, can we even figure out the amount of money we need for a child's college education ten or twenty years hence, much less save such an enormous sum?

In addition to the rapidly rising costs of raising children, a study of how adults and children use their time at home indicates that even teenagers today spend only a small amount of time on the kind of homemaking and child-care chores that make a substantial difference to the family standard of living. In general, most adolescents devote little time to family work, often much less than that of teenagers in other societies. While some adolescents continue to be pressed into service out of financial necessity, they neither earn significant amounts of money through paid work nor participate substantially in the work of the home.

Even beyond the direct costs of food, clothing, medical care, and education, children affect the family pocketbook in more indirect and long-term ways. Because of the time women devote to child rearing, children decrease the earnings and earning potential

of their mothers. Children represent economic opportunities forgone. Although more mothers are in the
labor force than at any other time in history, most
women continue to take time off before and after the
birth of their babies and tend to limit their work hours
during their years of child rearing. As a result, children
can be viewed as an economic liability, considerably
decreasing the amount of money their mothers can
expect to earn in their lifetimes.

Although there thus are few financial advantages to
having children, it is, of course, always possible that
the investment a parent makes will lead to a return in
later life when adult children can offer parents help in
old age. Both in principle and in practice, this is still a
reasonable expectation. Children continue to be an
important source of emotional, pragmatic, and financial support to their elderly parents. However, although the advantages of having children to rely on
when one gets old may occur to some would-be parents, such future rewards are rarely a compelling reason to have children. Indeed, many parents are ambivalent about turning to their children for help and
reject the notion that the children ever will (or should
be expected to) pay them back for the time and energy
they have invested. For instance, when we asked one
mother what she expected from her children in the
future, she replied:

"I certainly hope they will respect me, just as they
do now. I also hope that they will always love me as a
mother. But I will certainly not expect any favors from
them because I have been their mother. . . . As I go to
old age, if my husband dies, I think I could take care
of myself, even if I lived in a room in a house. I

wouldn't want to live with my children. I think they need their privacy, and I think I would need mine. So I would not expect a lot of them. If they turn out to be millionaires, it would be nice if they dropped me a few thousand every now and then. But other than that, I would just as soon they grow up, get good jobs, get married, have families, and invite me to dinner every once in a while. I don't expect them to pay me back. I had the children. I like the children. So I don't expect any reward."

In sum, economic reasons alone cannot account for why adults continue to undertake the responsibilities of child rearing. The reasons for and the rewards inherent in parenting have to be explained in more personal terms, by looking at how children contribute to the social, emotional, and moral lives of their parents.

People who wish to be parents usually realize that helping children grow into responsible and mature adults has the potential for satisfactions and joys that are difficult to equal in almost any other human endeavor. That such rewards are present is illustrated in the responses of two parents to the question, "What do you enjoy most about being a mother?"

"I enjoy my children. I enjoy the satisfaction. They're growing up nicely. I'm happy with them, and I'm proud that I've had a hand in it. I mean, a lot of it was them, but my husband and I tried hard and I'm proud."

"I feel my husband and I try so hard to do what we think is right and to give our children the kinds of things we should. We know we've given up certain things, but we've made that choice and we're glad that we've made any sacrifices we have. We can already see that we will get good results, where we can say all that work was worth it. The persistence and perseverance, that's what I'm proud of. That we've worked on problems hard and tried to resolve them and now we can see some of them work out well."

Children provide parents with new eyes on the world. Parents frequently remark on the opportunities they gain by sharing their children's insights into what is and what might be. Parents get pleasure and satisfaction from helping their children grow into the types of adults they want them to be. Mothers and fathers have definite ideas about the types of youngsters they want to raise. As one mother explained, "I would like to feel that my children have a place in their lives for God. I don't feel it has to be talked about, but I would also like to think they have a feeling of wanting to do for others, to think of others and not just of themselves all the time." While children certainly do not always live up to all their parents' expectations and ideals, more often than not the older generation gets to enjoy some of the fruits of its labors.

Even beyond this level of personal satisfaction, children provide their parents with a link to the future. In one of his movies, Woody Allen complains that he spends hours every day face-to-face with his own mortality. This sentiment probably makes little sense to most parents. It is not only that parents have little time to worry about their mortality when they are surrounded by active and demanding youngsters, it is also that children enhance their parents' stake and investment in the future. We recognize that our children will inherit the world we are planning and making for them now, and that they will inhabit it long after we have gone. Parents thus see a vivid expression of their own future as well as the future of the world in their children. One mother we know recalls how she was listening to a talk show one day while out on a family excursion. The topic was the development of a nuclear power plant in a neighboring community. During a heated exchange, an elderly participant said, "All you people who are opposed to this power plant, you all talk about the year 2000. I won't even be alive then." This mother reports that she turned in her seat and looked at her sleeping children and had to control an almost physical reflex to clutch them to her in order to protect them from this anonymous person who did not worry that they would be alive in the year 2000. This vision of one's children, of a part of oneself, existing in the future, is an essential part of parenting. It gives parents a sense of urgency to contribute to a better world as well as forming a stronger link to both past and future generations.

Unfortunately, such a vision of the future can be as disturbing as it is reassuring. One mother we interviewed summed up the feelings of many others when she expressed these reservations about taking on the responsibility of raising children today:

"I just wonder whether I should have had four children at all, because of the world we live in. I'm wondering, What are we offering them? What is so wonderful for them that I say it's the future? What is the future? But then I think that people had children during the terrible times of the Second World War, under the worst conditions. Yet people still fell in love, still wanted to be married, and still wanted to have children. So maybe that's the hope for the future. But I can't say I haven't thought of the whole nuclear threat, the whole world the way it is, and the way inflation is. What kind of life is it going to be for our children? I don't know whether my children are going to have the same standard of living that we have. We always thought in this country that each generation is going to have a better standard of living. I know my mother wished that for us. I know we hoped that our children would have more."

In a changing, complicated world, parents not only wonder if they can give their children a better life, they also question whether they will be able to take a stand and articulate their values in ways that are not outdated, that make sense to their children and yet are honest to themselves. Mothers and fathers often feel unsupported as they attempt to transmit to their offspring the values they feel are important. One reason for this lack of support is that families today tend to have looser ties to those social organizations we have depended upon to express and make visible our most cherished values and goals. Large extended families of grandparents, brothers, sisters, aunts, uncles, and cousins are often geographically dispersed and meet infrequently. Church membership is on the decline, and congregations in general are growing older as fewer families with young children become involved. An additional and related reason is that many of our traditional values are in flux. There is disagreement about what is right and what is wrong; about the proper roles of men and women; about the place of families, of religion, and of neighborhoods and communities in our lives. There are many times that parents feel at odds with society as they try to impress values on their children. As a result, parents become fearful that children will be exposed to the wrong influences and be led astray by peers and other outside forces parents cannot control. They express concern about the level of violence to which their children are exposed when they watch television, go to the movies, or even read magazines and newspapers. As one mother put it, "I feel like other people, too many other people, are making my daughter. It's like we have nothing to do with bringing her up, and this disturbs me. And I don't know how to stop it."

Parents feel that all too often they are caught in the middle. On the one hand, if they control their children's access to the outside world to too great an extent, they may leave the children friendless and unprepared for the world they eventually must live in as adults. On the other hand, if they allow greater freedom, they may be relinquishing their opportunity to discipline and train their youngsters as they would like.

For better or worse, children force parents to confront their own values and way of life in simple, everyday terms and situations. How old should a child be before he or she is allowed to date? What should children be told when they ask about premarital sex, birth control, smoking, or alcohol and other drugs? How much should children be encouraged or forced to go to church, to visit their grandparents, to help out around the house? Frequently, parents are uncertain about the correct answers to such questions. They are left feeling like wanderers in a moral never-never land. At times they find themselves allowing, encouraging, and even planning activities about which they have reservations.

In a social environment that can be frightening and threatening, it is difficult for parents to know how to protect their children. What can be done about the increases in juvenile crime, crimes by adults against children, and even crimes of children against children? Most parents acknowledge that children cannot be protected against every ill wind that blows. Yet how can parents know what types of activities and exposures are healthy and helpful to children and what kinds are generally destructive? How can parents find the right compromise between the need to protect children from painful experiences and the need to allow them the breathing space necessary for them to gain independence and maturity?

In an era of considerable ambiguity about values and about the responsibilities of parenthood, it is increasingly difficult for mothers and fathers to draw the line between caring and protecting, on the one hand, and fostering independence and growth, on the other. For many parents, particularly those living in cities, this tension is reflected in the differences they detect between the way they were raised a generation ago and the way they feel compelled to raise their children now. One mother reported, "When I was six years old, I went shopping for my mother, walked to school and to my friends' homes by myself. On a summer evening I might stay out until eight or nine o'clock. My mother would know that I was in the neighborhood, but she didn't need to know exactly where I was, and our games of hide-and-seek might range over several blocks. But now I find that I, like all the other mothers

who live around here, walk with my child to school, to
the store, to her friends' homes, unless I know that
some other parent will be doing it in my place." This
mother is saddened that she cannot follow the patterns
by which she was raised and still provide the protection she feels her child needs today. Such experiences
serve as stark reminders of the kind of world we live in
and the kind of world our children will inherit.

As parents try to face the moral and ethical dilemmas
posed by raising children in modern times, they find
their own doubts and ambivalence reflected in pain-
fully revealing ways. This is at once one of the most
exciting and rewarding aspects of child rearing as well
as one of the most difficult and challenging. Children
tend to see all the ways in which their parents' behaviors contradict their avowed beliefs, and they don't
hesitate to point out these contradictions and hypoc-
risies in both direct and covert ways. Parents thus find
themselves scrutinized by their children. In turn, they
are able to scrutinize themselves through the eyes of a
younger and less jaded generation. Children are continually probing—little scientists of morality that they
are—to find out if the ethical world their parents present is real and dependable. Parents find themselves
having to define and redefine their own values and
way of life in response to this careful scrutiny.

Children thus open up vistas that adults never imagined before becoming parents. Children force their
parents to uncover hidden strengths and truths about
themselves in response to the challenges of child rearing. Adults even find themselves changing their ways
to reflect the values they wish to pass on to their
children. Whether this means that parents give up

smoking or cursing or make more heroic efforts, children often force parents to live up to their moral code. Raising children is a continual process of learning and discovery. It not only provides parents with a personal and intimate understanding of how a human life unfolds but compels them to come to a new understanding of what is important in their own lives, of who they are and what they truly value.

HOW CHILDREN AFFECT THE DIFFERENT SPHERES OF THEIR PARENTS' LIVES

Although we have discussed some of the pressures and tensions and some of the rewards and benefits of having children, it is clear that youngsters affect their parents' lives in many more tangible ways. Because child rearing is a time-consuming as well as a physically and emotionally draining responsibility, children have an enormous impact on the lives of the adults responsible for them. This impact spreads far beyond the confines of the family home and incorporates almost every aspect of a parent's life.

Since the relationship between employment and family life has received a great deal of attention over the past two decades, the workplace is probably the first setting that comes to mind when we think about how the lives of adults are affected by the presence of children. We will devote considerably more time to this topic later, but it is important here to acknowledge the extent to which the responsibility for children changes not only how parents feel about their paid jobs and careers but also the actual patterns of their paid work involvements.

The rise of maternal employment, in particular, has sparked much public interest and concern; many of us have strong feelings about how children, women, and families are affected when mothers take jobs outside the home. Unfortunately, many media presentations as well as much of the research on maternal employment have left women feeling damned if they do and damned if they don't. On the one hand, homemakers often complain, even when they feel they have made a good and conscientious choice to stay with their young children, that the women's movement has made them feel unliberated. They feel their unpaid domestic labors have been devalued. Such women express concern that other people see them as unproductive, if not irresponsible, members of society. On the other hand, sufficient doubts have been raised about the possible detrimental effects of maternal employment that employed mothers are also often confused and feel conflicted about what they should be doing. Even when their income is essential to their families, many working mothers worry about how their jobs will affect their children's development and well-being. Given these contradictory messages, women find it difficult to sort through their own feelings about motherhood and employment and come up with a plan that seems workable and beneficial to their children, their families, and ultimately to themselves.

While the changes in women's employment have been dramatic and there has been more talk about women's changing roles both in the workplace and at home, men too have been affected by changing times. More often than not, today's fathers want to be intimately involved in their children's lives and, starting with participation in the childbirth experience, to be active parents. It is not always easy, however, for them to follow through on their convictions. Traditionally responsible for earning enough money to support family life, fathers find that the pressure to earn a big and steady salary increases throughout the child-rearing period. At the same time that they might want to be spending more time with their children, fathers feel a growing pressure to work long hours, to seek job advancement, and to devote as much time as possible to their wage-earning activities. In recognition of these often-conflicting demands, this predicament has been termed the "male life cycle squeeze."

Therefore, just as women typically are drawn out of the labor force when they have children, fathers find themselves increasingly pulled in. It is hard for couples to find a good solution to the problems both mothers and fathers experience when they try to combine parenthood and employment. Particularly in times of inflation and high unemployment, it can be agonizingly difficult for fathers to figure out a reasonable way to earn enough money and still have sufficient time and energy left over for family responsibilities. Conversely, it can be equally difficult for mothers to figure out how much time they really need to spend with their children and how much time they can devote to their jobs and to furthering their careers. While we cannot hope to offer perfect solutions to these complex questions, we think it is helpful to provide examples of how other families have worked out solutions and how other mothers and fathers think about the relation between their paid jobs and their unpaid family work.

In addition to affecting their parents' interactions in

the workplace, children also embed their mothers and
fathers in the larger social world. Adults find that
having children alters their relations with their families, their neighborhoods, and their communities. It is
not only how adults think of themselves but how they
are seen by others that changes with the birth of their
first child. One father reported that when he took his
wife to the hospital he was a boy and when he returned
home, with his wife and new child, he was an adult.
Having children is viewed as the ultimate adult responsibility. Even those to whom we are closest are
likely to change their vision of us once we become
mothers and fathers. With parenthood, we become full
members of our families and our communities, com-
plete with the responsibilities and privileges that such
memberships entail.

Most men and women report that they became closer
to their own parents when they became parents themselves, both because of the understanding they now
share of what it means to be a parent and because of
the shared love both feel for the new generation. For
grandparents as well as parents, the new generation is
a vision of the future, a part of what is to come that one
can directly influence and help through one's own
actions and interventions. Brothers and sisters, aunts
and uncles, and even more distant relatives of new
parents may also feel an investment in the young, and
this sense of shared commitment can have a big impact
on adult's feelings of belonging to an extended family.

In addition to these family changes, parents also find
that their other social worlds change dramatically as
children grow. From the first moment a woman knows
she is pregnant, she is likely to be more drawn to other

mothers and to feel a special kinship with them because of their shared experience. Then, when children are old enough to have their own social lives, their friends' families often become a part of their parents' social lives as well. Families with children the same age share many similar concerns and problems; they are likely to take pleasure and find companionship in many of the same events and activities. Parents seek and get support from one another, whether it be in the form of parent support groups or through chance encounters at the park. Parents also find themselves becoming committed to the kind of work it takes to turn a neighborhood into a place where one would like to raise children. Furthermore, the responsibility of parenting leads men and women into different activities in the larger community. Because of their desire to make sure their children get what they need, parents are likely to become involved in schools, in neighborhood and community action projects, and in the myriad of community groups that serve families, from churches to associations such as the Scouts, sports teams, and child-care organizations. Thus, children pull men and women into new social engagements and provide the impetus for adults to become invested and active in the social life of their community. As a number of surveys indicate, men and women in the active child-rearing years are more likely to be involved in their neighborhoods and communities than are adults at any other stage of the life course.

The final and perhaps most important way children affect parents is by changing the nature of their marriages. The time a couple can spend together, as well as the emotional ties between the individuals of the marriage dyad, are affected by the birth of a baby. Many new parents report that they never imagined how different their family life would be once they had a child. Most feel that no one could possibly have warned them of all the differences an infant could make—they never would have believed it. On the one hand, children create a new and powerful focus of emotions; they bring a new significance to the marriage relationship. They are constant reminders of the importance of loving and caring, of consideration and communication. But there is no denying that children also create enormous pressures. In most relationships, long before children arrive on the scene, adults have worked out some mechanisms for settling differences, for deciding what to do next, for dealing with each other when either spouse is tired, grumpy, or unhappy. All these strategies are put to the ultimate test once children appear. All of a sudden, there is less time to be together, less time to negotiate, less time to work out problems. As one mother complained, "The children really want to devour our time together; they want all our time and our attention."

In many ways, children are a mixed blessing to a marriage. Along with the strains and pressures they create come the special shared moments, shared joys, and shared pride. The more that couples are able to be flexible and deal with the unpredictability of life with children, the more likely their marriage not only will survive but will be enriched by their mutual investment in child rearing. For example, one mother we spoke with talked of how she and her husband incorporated their children into their marriage:

"I'd say my husband and I get along very well. We

definitely have our disagreements. I don't agree with everything he says. We argue; we have healthy arguments. But I don't hide the arguments at all from the two boys. Because I think it's just the way of life. I don't care who you are—everybody argues. There has to be something wrong with you if you never argue; things just don't go that smoothly all the time. So I think my boys should see both sides of it. I think they should see the affection and I think they should see the disenchantment, too. I think they shouldn't have the mistaken idea that marriage is a fairy tale, that having children is a fairy tale. Everybody should see the ups and downs of it. There is dissatisfaction whatever you do, but it shouldn't outweigh the good."

In essence, this book is about the ups and downs, the satisfactions and disenchantments of having children, of raising a family in modern times. In the following chapters, we try to point out ways parents can think about the sometimes overwhelming and contradictory needs of children at the same time that they respond to their own adult needs and commitments. Although no book can begin to cover the diversity and range of responses parents have to child rearing, we discuss some of the most important issues men and women face as they take on the exciting but often perplexing and complicated task of raising the next generation.

CHAPTER 2

The Entry to Parenthood

The birth of a baby marks a major transition point, what some psychologists have even labeled a crisis, in the lives of adults. Becoming a parent means taking on a major new life role. In the months surrounding a baby's birth, parents find themselves redefining and adapting their way of life to fit the demands of child rearing. They readjust their life-styles, their work patterns, their self-perceptions, and their way of interacting with others. The entry to parenthood marks a time when almost everything about a person's life is in transition. New parents often are drained and confused by the sheer number of adjustments they must make. At the same time, they are exhilarated and propelled forward by the prospect of watching their infants pass the milestones of the first year, from that first rewarding smile to those first faltering steps.

One of the paradoxes of parenting is that it is at once both the most private and the most public of experiences. Having a baby not only changes what goes on within the private domain of the family, it also transforms relationships between the newly expanded family and the outside world. Fortunately, considering the emotional and physical strains of infant care, few parents actually are required to raise a child entirely on their own. Parenting is rarely a solo experience. Instead, probably more than at any other time in their adult lives, mothers and fathers rely on the help and advice of those they trust, including relatives, friends, and neighbors as well as such professionals as obstetricians, pediatricians, and ministers. As they turn to others for help in coping with their new responsibilities, parents become increasingly aware of the importance of their social networks, of the people they can count on to lend a helping hand. It can be very reassuring to know that others are available when aid is needed. Not surprisingly, those new parents who are most isolated from others typically find it the most difficult to adjust to their new role. New parents who have recently moved to a new community and single parents with a recently disrupted family life can find the burdens of parenting particularly heavy. Grandma volunteering to provide a few hours of unexpected baby-sitting; a neighbor dropping off a casserole for dinner during the first week that mother and baby are home from the hospital; a friend with two children of her own calling to find out how things are going and lending a sympathetic ear—all these add up to making parents feel supported.

But the benefits of having others to rely on do not come without some costs; friendships or close ties with relatives are not handed to us on a silver platter. Maintaining personal relationships and sustaining a network one can draw upon as needed requires work. Even as parents are challenged by what can seem to be the overwhelming and incessant demands of an infant, they find themselves having to redefine many of their personal ties: with one another as a couple, with their parents and in-laws, and with many other members of their social networks. One of the major strains of the early months of parenting is the effort it takes to forge these new social relationships. In this chapter, we look at how the social worlds of adults evolve as they become parents, and how parents experience the stresses and rewards of this transition period of their lives.

BETWEEN HUSBANDS AND WIVES: NEW STRAINS AND REWARDS

At a time when so many marriages are ending in divorce and so many women are being left to raise children without the support of a husband, it is no wonder that couples worry about how a baby will affect their marriage. How will the entry of a third person into their home and hearts affect a couple's ability to remain confidants and lovers? Will there be enough time for each other once the baby is around? In short, does a baby cement or undermine a marriage?

There are still no clear-cut answers to these questions. Divorce statistics show that couples with young children are less likely to split up than either couples without children or couples whose children have grown. Yet it is difficult to know whether this reflects marital contentment during the early child-rearing years or just the considerable difficulties and expense of going through a divorce and establishing separate households when young children are involved. Do couples with young children stay married because they want to or because they have to?

Couples with young children usually report that they are less satisfied with their marriage than are childless couples. The presence of children does indeed seem to reduce marital satisfaction, particularly among women. New parents acknowledge a number of problems: they talk about fatigue, the lack of time to talk over problems, the lack of energy left over to nurture and care for each other once they have cared for the baby, and so on. But despite these problems they go on to talk about the added sense of shared pleasure and accomplishment that parenting brings to a marriage. Mothers and fathers report that, yes, having a baby does make life harder; yes, it is more of an effort to find the space to enjoy each other; and, yes, parenting can be a hassle. Yet for most the extra work and effort seems worth it. A happy, growing baby is something real and rewarding to show for one's labors.

While it may be difficult to prove that having a baby makes a marriage stronger, there is little argument that it makes the marriage different. There are couples who thrive on this difference; there are others who don't. One reason it is difficult to generalize is that the timing and circumstances of a first child's birth are so variable. Some couples get married precisely because they want to have children; others decide to have a baby only after years of deliberation. There are those who carefully time their families, and everything works out; others may experience prolonged periods of infertility and even a miscarriage or two before a successful delivery, late but expected; still others are caught off guard and have to adjust to the unplanned-for addition. Certainly these variations, as well as whether or not a man and woman agree it is a good time to start a family, contribute to whether becoming parents has a positive or negative effect on a marriage.

Despite this range of parenting experiences, it is possible to point out some basic similarities in how infants affect their parents' marriages. First, it is an inescapable fact of life that the pressures of parenting take something away from the resources that couples have to invest in each other. One mother described the problem this way:

"Taking care of our son takes so much energy; our focus is on this third person a great deal of the time. So a lot of things that we would have caught earlier— conflicts, let's say—go by the wayside. You put them all on the back burner because you've got this other person to deal with. Then, before you know it, your problems have blown up. Our feeling is that we just don't have the time to get to our own issues, and therefore problems really get much bigger than they ever have before. We aren't able to catch them early on, like when there were just the two of us."

Most new parents expect to be pressed for time. They are prepared for this change, at least on an intellectual level. In childbirth classes, in casual talks with other parents, and just by observing other mothers and fathers, expectant parents learn a lot about what it takes to cope with an infant and a marriage at the same time. In addition, couples today reap the benefits of more open discussions of how pregnancy, childbirth, and nursing an infant may affect a woman's sexual desire, and husbands are encouraged to be responsive and sympathetic to their wives' changing physical and emotional states. Prospective fathers as well as mothers are counseled about what to expect when the baby arrives.

But all the advance preparation in the world goes only so far to prepare couples for the changes that actually occur. It is often impossible for couples to imagine the strength of the feelings they will have for their baby or how fatigued a new parent can feel after a twenty-four-hour stint of baby tending. It is not only the actual work involved that is tiring; babies also have a knack for sapping their parents' emotional and physical reserves. A nonparent can hardly imagine how depleted one feels after rocking little Susie for what seems like forever to keep her from crying, nursing and changing her every three hours, and in countless other small ways trying to provide emotional and physical comfort for her. The last thing many mothers want to do at the end of such a day (or, for that matter, many of those fathers who care for small children) is respond to a spouse's emotional needs or sexual approaches. In fact, each of us seems to have a "touch" limit, a threshold of how much physical contact we can tolerate on any given day. Babies often force us to go beyond this limit, leaving no reserve for adult contact. Feeling so depleted is not a personal flaw, it is a part of being human. As much as books advise parents to save special times for each other, often there aren't enough hours in the day or week. Adult personal needs sometimes have to be overlooked in order to meet the demands of the baby. One of the toughest challenges parents face is to strike a balance between their own needs—as individuals and as a couple—and the needs of their offspring. Starting in this first year of parenting, couples must develop a child-rearing style that complements their marriage.

One thing to take into account in experimenting with different arrangements is the temperament and personality of one's son or daughter. Not all infants have the same needs or place the same demands on their parents. A baby's disposition and emotional makeup can have a profound effect on the experiences of new parents. For example, some babies are just plain easier than others: they sleep and eat regularly, they are alert and active enough to make playtime rewarding, and they are responsive to their parents' efforts to calm and soothe them. Other babies are more difficult: they are cranky or colicky, they are off-schedule, they rarely sleep for long periods of time, or they are harder to cuddle or to engage in play. Whether babies are difficult or easy often has little to do with their parents' care; babies are just born with different skills and styles of interacting. Yet how easily a child fits into the household routine certainly affects how readily couples can adapt to parenthood. It is impossible to know ahead of time what kind of baby one will get—this is one of the true surprises of parenting. It is also one of the reasons why being a good parent means remaining flexible, prepared to deal not with some textbook-perfect baby but with the special, distinctive personality who enters your home.

Many pediatricians feel that this element of surprise is essential to good parenting. Some even advise mothers who undergo amniocentesis to forgo the available knowledge of their children's sex. They fear that when parents have facts as well as dreams about their as yet unborn children, their expectations of that child become both more stereotyped and more fixed. For instance, parents informed in the fourth or fifth month of pregnancy that they will have a girl might well begin to imagine a relatively placid, petite, and feminine individual. When their little girl turns out to be noisy and rambunctious, quick to learn and quick to express herself, they may find themselves unnecessarily embattled with their new infant, not because she is difficult or unusual but because she is different from what they imagined.

In sum, together with the problems and difficulties a baby introduces into a marriage come the satisfactions and pleasures that couples experience as they share in molding a new life and experiencing a new life stage.

DIVIDING THE WORK: NEW ROLES AND DEMANDS

One of the most basic agreements couples make is to decide who is responsible for doing what household chores and who is responsible for providing the money necessary to support family life. That is, they decide how to divide the labor involved in maintaining a home and family. Whatever agreement couples may have reached before they became parents needs to be renegotiated once a baby enters the picture.

There have been many studies of the division of labor between husbands and wives, and virtually all have reached the same conclusion: Having a baby pressures both men and women into assuming less egalitarian and more sex-stereotyped employment and family roles. Even as many women are striving to make a place for themselves in the world of employment and many men are struggling to become actively involved in the upbringing of their children, the presence of a baby is what most often forces couples into more traditional roles as mothers and fathers, homemakers and employees.

The vast majority of women work far into their pregnancies, and all but a relative few expect to return to full-time employment as their children grow older. However, most stop working to become full-time homemakers, at least for a while. In contrast, only a small minority of fathers take off more than a couple of days from their jobs to provide baby care. Even in countries such as Sweden where men are given the opportunity to take paid paternity leaves, it is women who typically take the time off from their jobs to provide full-time child care. Careful scrutiny of national labor force participation statistics shows that although women are spending a greater portion of their lives employed than ever before, they are still spending some time being mothers and homemakers.

The amount of time a woman decides to spend at home depends on such considerations as how much her family relies on her income, how great an investment she has already made in her education and career, and even on whether or not she is able to find other women to keep her company there. Some women enjoy the experience of full-time parenting and find they want to stay home longer with their babies than they had expected. They extend their maternity leaves, quit the jobs they thought they might want to return to, or make similar arrangements for more prolonged stints as full-time homemakers. Still others find that being a mother and homemaker is too confining, and they return to work not only for the income but for the social and intellectual satisfactions the workplace offers. Mothers with young children often report that they really didn't know how long they wanted to remain at home until after they had tried it. Feelings can and do change after a baby's birth, and their advice to other women is to remain open to new arrangements.

Women also at times feel that there is no really "perfect" solution to the problem of combining a career and child rearing. An article in *The Wall Street Journal*, Sept. 7, 1983, describes the dilemmas of mothers caught between highly valued occupations and their desires to be with their children.

> Barbara Keck, who has an M.B.A. from Harvard University, was earning $35,000 a year as a division manager at a Stamford, Conn., manufacturing concern when she gave birth to a son in 1979. Mrs. Keck says she "fully intended" to return to work in two weeks. But after Martin's birth, Mrs. Keck took six weeks off to enjoy him more. And when she finally did go back to work, she lasted only two weeks.
>
> "I just couldn't pick up the schedule," Mrs. Keck says. Awakening at 6:30 a.m., she rode the train for an hour from New York City to Stamford, spent her lunch hour feeding the baby, who stayed with a sitter in Stamford, and got home at 8 p.m. Exhausted, Mrs. Keck asked her employer for part-time hours. When the company refused, she quit.
>
> "I felt a split loyalty," Mrs. Keck says. "I had built up a fair amount of respect for myself there. But I realized that (the company) wasn't going to be there when I was on my deathbed and the rattle was in my throat. There is plenty of time to do the career, but children are small for a very short time."

After finding out how much effort it takes to combine jobs and child rearing, many women find themselves resenting and rejecting the image of "supermom," the woman who does it all. They begin to formulate more realistic plans for doing now what they think is important now. They recognize that their priorities changed when they became parents, just as they probably will change again as their children grow older. This recognition of one's life course, of one's potential for change and openness to new experiences, is one of the positive outcomes of having children.

Regardless of the actual arrangements they make and how long they remain out of the labor force, there are some similarities in how women feel about their jobs once they become mothers. In an age that emphasizes the importance of employment, it is striking how many mothers with young children continue to put their responsibilities to parenting first. They adapt their work patterns and schedules to fit their child-care responsibilities and the value they place on being home for their children. Far more women than men work part-time hours, for example, or take short-term jobs, interchanging time at home with time at work.

For many couples the shift in a woman's priorities from employment to homemaking appears to make the most economic sense. It is not just because most women are more comfortable assuming a greater share of the parenting role and most men are more comfortable taking on a greater share of the breadwinner role (since these are the roles their own mothers and fathers generally assumed). It is also because this division of labor usually makes more financial sense from an individual couple's point of view. On average, women continue to earn far less than men per hour worked; most wives earn considerably less than their husbands, even before the birth of a baby. It therefore seems financially wise for the mother to decrease her work hours, particularly if her earned income would be spent largely on the associated costs of employment such as child care.

When they feel they have the choice, many couples still prefer to have at least one parent home most of the time and available to provide child care. Women, in particular, report how they want to spend as much time as possible with their children while they are very young. "They grow so fast, you just want to be there to see everything," one woman told us, and her response echoes the sentiments expressed by many of the other mothers with whom we have spoken. "I can give Timothy something no one else can," another woman explained. "That's why I make it a point to be here for him." At times, it is women who have spent a number of years already working who feel the strongest pull toward staying home. "I did what I could with my job, and now I'm ready to be home for a while," reported a social worker who was planning to return to work within the next few years.

Interestingly, women talk about wanting to be home with their babies both because of what children may gain from having constant, daily contact with their mothers and because of what they themselves get from the experience of parenting. Having the option to combine employment and child care, many women choose to stay home—at least for a prescribed period of time around the births of their children.

There are, of course, women who stay on their jobs,

just as they did before becoming mothers. For some, this decision is based more on constraint than on choice. They need their jobs to support their families—in fact, they often need better-paying jobs or longer hours than the ones they currently have. Other women do have more of the luxury of working by choice, because of their desire to pursue the careers they had before giving birth. They search out infant day-care programs or family day-care homes, or leave their babies with relatives while they go to work. In some two-parent families, the wife's income is recognized as equal in significance to that of the husband. However, in other families where new mothers remain employed or take only relatively short maternity leaves, couples tend to start viewing a wife's income as supplementary rather than as essential.

Even in those families where mothers, as well as fathers, remain employed during the early months of their children's lives, mothers tend to assume a significantly larger share of the work of parenting. Just as women are far more likely, even when they are employed, to undertake more of the housework, they also do more feeding, bathing, diapering, and rocking to sleep.

We can see many reasons why women are pulled into this domestic pattern: the ease of falling back on traditional roles, the realities of the labor market, the importance many couples continue to place on having at least one parent at home, and the satisfactions and pleasures many women experience as full-time mothers. With the birth of a baby, then, the importance of women's jobs tends to be downplayed while the importance of their contributions to parenting is high-lighted.

In contrast to the experience of women, men find their time increasingly invested in the world of employment. Many fathers report that having a child made them feel more tied down to their jobs and more responsible for providing the family income. If having a baby limits what women feel they can accomplish in their careers, it also often limits the choices and freedom of men. Men complain that they are less able to take chances, to quit a job they don't like, or to start over in a new field once they become fathers. At times they feel caught up in a career rat race they had hoped to avoid.

The patterns we have described sound familiar, since they fit traditional concepts of "men's work" and "women's work." Yet, they can also seem incongruous with modern times, out of step with what couples wanted or expected from their lives. While some men and women adapt to their new roles with little trouble, others experience great discomfort. Women, especially, may feel conflicted about leaving their jobs or sacrificing to any major extent the careers they struggled to create. Men may feel trapped in jobs they don't like and prevented from spending as much time as they want with their children.

When both husbands and wives are employed, mothers may feel relieved from the tensions of losing the investment in their career, and fathers may feel somewhat more relaxed about their own career development. However, mothers, and fathers too, will often feel conflicted about the necessity for leaving children in the care of someone else. It also can be difficult for working couples to decide on a division of homemaking and child-care chores that does not depend overwhelmingly on the wife's contributions.

Unfortunately, it is very easy for new parents to start blaming each other for the discrepancies between expectations and reality, for the lack of a good fit between what they want to be doing and the work that needs to be done. In order to prevent this from occurring, husbands and wives often find it helpful to recognize and talk about the constraints on each other's lives. They then can start working toward an arrangement and division of labor that more closely fits their personal needs and goals. It is helpful for them, in doing so, to recognize the extent to which having a baby results in shifts in the amount of power or control that husbands and wives exert over different spheres of their marriages.

MARRIAGE AND POWER

In any relationship between two individuals, there is always a balance of power, an agreement (stated or not) about who is responsible for what, who is in charge of making what decisions. In changing the division of labor between husbands and wives, a baby's presence threatens the established and delicate balance of power. For instance, when women stop bringing home a paycheck or when their earnings substantially decrease in relation to those of their husbands, women often report that they feel powerless. They are suddenly uncomfortable making any financial decisions; they feel as though they are now spending "his" money, not their own. They may also feel less able to stand up for their rights in the marriage, more vulnerable to their husbands' decisions and whims. As one woman complained, "I feel more dependent upon him, because I'm not out there doing my own thing anymore."

While the most obvious shift in power is away from wives and toward breadwinning husbands, who are bringing home more money, there is also a more subtle shift of power operating in the opposite direction. As wives take on more of the housework and child care, husbands may see themselves as locked out of domestic decisions. They may start to feel like intruders in their own homes. "I'd help out more but she never thinks I do anything right" is a common complaint of husbands who feel powerless in this arena.

One reason for highlighting the role of power (or the lack of it) in a marriage is that it is important for new parents to realize the implications of such power shifts and the problems they may cause. For example, it helps if new mothers and fathers take the time to talk about how they value their own work and that of their spouses. Just what economic value does the couple place on the wife's contribution to housework and homemaking? If she is continuing to earn an income, is her economic contribution valued? Does a husband appreciate his wife's labor, whether or not she brings home a paycheck? If the man is charged with providing most of the financial support, in what way is the woman also supporting the family? Whose money is it: *his, hers,* or *theirs?* Conversely, are a husband's efforts and attempts to pitch in around the house and with the baby consistently devalued? Every time he tries to help out, is he told he is doing something wrong?

Unfortunately, the first time some couples start discussing these issues is with a marriage counselor or even in a divorce hearing as outsiders try to sort out the dynamics of the marriage and who is responsible for contributing what. How much better for couples to recognize earlier that power issues are important and that the shifts in power that usually accompany a baby's birth can shake up the foundations of a marriage.

In addition to talking about personal values, it is also helpful for couples to acknowledge that more than just personalities are at stake when some of these difficulties arise. Rather, it is the structure of contemporary work and family roles that actually creates some problems. It is hard to be home with a baby most of the day, just as it is hard to feel pressured to provide enough money to keep the family going. It is also staggeringly hard to combine child-rearing responsibilities and jobs in a twenty-four-hour day. Parents need to feel supported by their spouses as they adjust to their new roles as mothers and fathers and to a new division of labor. Couples benefit when they make the time to talk with each other about the sheer amount of work that needs to be done to care for an infant and about the importance of the unpaid work necessary to maintain a family. They need to keep in touch with how they are feeling about the changes in their lives. Talking about these issues prevents problems from festering and damaging a marriage, just as it helps new mothers and fathers to deal with their lives and the stresses caused by a baby. It also helps them prepare for the future. Couples who are successful in opening these lines of communication are the ones who are likely to report that the depth of their communication, their knowledge of each other, actually increased after they became parents.

In short, new parents fare best when they take the time to discuss and work out arrangements for getting done the added work caused by the addition of a baby to the household. The specific division of labor between husbands and wives (that is, whether the woman remains a homemaker and the man the sole provider or whether both share more equally in housework and employment) seems to be no more important than the couple's satisfaction and comfort with their current work styles. This research finding suggests how important it is for mothers and fathers to talk about their roles and the changes in their lives brought about by the birth of a baby. Working out a way to talk to each other about how things are going, about the satisfactions as well as the pressures and problems of child rearing, is one of the most critical new tasks people face as they become parents.

Husbands and wives need to recognize that these discussions and negotiations are part of the work of parenting. Time and energy must be allotted for communication. Unfortunately, it is hard for new parents to find this time in their daily lives. For example, employed mothers of young children may feel that their lives are so filled by the daily round of responsibilities that there is not time or energy left to even think about renegotiating the work load of the home or to discuss alternatives for the organization of family life. But finding time and working toward a mutually acceptable solution goes a long way toward helping couples cope with the demands of the early years of parenting at the same time that they are striving to sustain and improve their own relationship.

TRANSFORMING OTHER PERSONAL RELATIONSHIPS: THE PLACE OF GRANDPARENTS

In addition to redefining the marriage of their parents, children also transform the relationships of their mothers and fathers with their extended families. For example, many women report that they grew closer to their mothers after the birth of a child. On becoming mothers themselves, women often experience strong feelings of empathy with their own mothers, a mutual understanding of what motherhood is like. One mother recounted how powerful a sensation this can be.

"I remember vividly a dream I had while I was pregnant. I remember experiencing a sense of loss in this dream that my mother must have experienced as all of us left home. And it was the first time I had sort of an emotional realization of what it felt like to her. I mean, here I was just about ready to give birth, and that's like the first mini-loss, that's the first loss. That's the first change you have to deal with as a mother. And then there'll be tons more down the road, sort of culminating with when your child finally leaves and is an independent being totally. . . . If there's anything that sort of came to me in terms of understanding, it's just a greater sense of compassion for my mother, for other parents, now that I've sort of experienced this myself. There's a lot of stuff I guess I just understand differently now. All I can say is that becoming a mother gave me a greater sense of compassion. I feel a bit wiser about the whole thing, not so ready to lay guilt or blame. . . . I feel that I just have a deeper understanding of the difficulties my mother had."

In addition to strengthening the emotional bond between mothers and daughters, grandmothers are often called upon to help out in many material ways during the early child-rearing years. The amount of support they can provide clearly depends on a number of factors. Most important is, of course, how far away they live. But other considerations, such as whether or not they themselves have full-time jobs and how good their health is, also count. Even those women who live far away from their daughters, or who are in some way limited in the amount of time they have to visit, generally make a special effort to be on hand around the time of their grandchildren's births. Although more and more women may be turning to how-to books, friends, and even professionals for advice and information about pregnancy, childbirth, and child rearing, many still prefer to turn to their own mothers for aid and comfort when the going gets tough.

How involved a grandmother becomes in the new family is often a matter of personal style and reflects not only the history of the relationship between mother and daughter but also the marriage relationship between the new parents. Some couples prefer to keep grandparents somewhat at bay, particularly during the first few weeks after the baby's birth. They want the members of their own new family to be comfortable with one another before others come visiting. They prefer a definite boundary between themselves and the outside world, including close relatives. In such cases, husbands tend to provide the bulk of support to their wives during the difficult first weeks of juggling housework and infant care. In other families, the division of labor is more sex-stereotyped and the boundaries between the nuclear family and the extended family are more diffuse. Here it is grandmothers (or even sisters or aunts) who are expected to lend a helping hand. No matter how much actual support grandmothers provide, however, new mothers generally report feeling closer to their families once they begin a family of their own.

Some new mothers also grow closer to their fathers. They enjoy seeing them interact with their children. Often these daughters feel that their fathers did not play a very active role in their own upbringing because of the pressures of their jobs, the demands of military service, or some similar constraint. As men enter retirement, however, they often have more time to spend with children. As one mother reported:

"I've begun to see a side of my father I didn't see before. My dad was away a lot while we were being born and growing up. He never really spent much time around us. And now with his grandchildren coming and his own life changing—he's facing retirement—I can see him becoming very interested in little children and wanting to be able to relax and be there for his grandchildren." Another woman expressed her surprise that her father got so much pleasure from her young son that "now he'll just come over and let my mother and me go shopping while he stays with him. I think he is enjoying his grandchildren more than his own children."

This focus on women's relationships with kin reflects the reality that it is women more than men who serve as what has been termed the "kin keepers" of their families. By and large, wives take more responsibility than their husbands for phoning relatives, arranging visits and social get-togethers, buying presents for birthdays and Christmas, and the assorted other activities that go into being part of an active kin network. Women usually spend more time with relatives than do men. This is not to say that becoming a parent has little or no effect on how new fathers get along with their parents and in-laws. As the frequency of regular visits between generations rises with the birth of a grandchild, a man also often finds himself socializing more with members of his extended family than he did before becoming a parent. Men as well as women spend more time with relatives and think of their relatives as more important to them after they become parents.

This increased contact with relatives has some inherent problems. Men complain of the strain of having to work out new relationships with kinfolk as one of the major difficulties they experienced in becoming fathers. Women too can experience some stress as they try to renegotiate these relationships, particularly when their own values and infant-care strategies conflict with those of their parents or in-laws. Most new parents are concerned about their ability to deal with an infant appropriately and according to their own standards and values. Understandably, they are sensitive to criticism. Tensions may arise between the generations. Both mothers and fathers talk of how they needed some time to discover the right balance between involving their parents in their own lives and fostering their children's relationships with the grandparents, on the one hand, and maintaining a separate, independent household and marital harmony, on the other. Once again, this is a reminder that maintaining social relationships—whether a marriage or a relationship with kin—requires a good deal of effort. After taking care of the baby and trying to meet their own needs as a couple, new parents frequently have little energy in reserve. So it often takes some time before interactions with relatives reach a new level at which all are comfortable and satisfied.

THE IMPORTANCE OF COMMUNITY TIES

When men and women are employed full-time before they become parents, they often have little time or incentive to become involved in the daily happenings in their neighborhoods. "Oh, we don't know them, they're both working, and they're never around," was the description one mother gave of a childless couple on her block. "I didn't have the time to make any friends in the neighborhood," another woman explained, "until I was home with Marie." With the birth of their children, many couples, and women in particular, learn to appreciate and make greater use of their neighbors and neighborhoods.

In addition, several studies suggest that men are more likely to become involved in the daily activities of parenting and household chores if they have friends and acquaintances who play an active role at home. The opportunity to engage in conversation and share parenting experiences with other men provides encouragement and support for new fathers. Such support may be particularly valuable when colleagues at work do not readily understand the constraints on a father's time and energy.

The more time either parent spends at home, the more vital it is for him or her to meet others in the same situation. If a new mother is lucky enough to live in a neighborhood with other mothers, she often feels less isolated and has an easier time making the transition from full-time employment to being home for all or part of the day. If there are no neighbors with children, women often look for other ways to find new friends who share similar constraints and experiences. The first years of parenting are not always an easy time for the new parents to reach out to other people; it can be hard to get out of the house with a baby and difficult to search out new groups of people. But many parents find it is a necessity.

Fortunately there are a number of places to turn. For example, some churches sponsor mothers' groups or special events which parents and babies can attend together. Other parents try to maintain contacts they made during childbirth classes. Still others find someone to chat with at the local park or recreation area. Searching out other new parents takes some effort, but usually the results are worth the energy invested. New parents can feel dislocated and cut off from peers, and these feelings can give rise to depression and discontent with the parental role. Having friends who understand what they are going through and who can lend an ear or a hand really helps mothers and fathers get through the tough times at home with the new baby. In time, it gets easier to get out of the house, and children themselves start pulling their parents into new friendships and networks. But the importance of having others with whom to share the parenting experience is obvious right from the start. Parenting is a tough road to travel alone, and in the early weeks and months of their children's lives, most parents discover what it means to count on others and to share their experience.

CHAPTER 3

The Preschool Years:
The Fleeting Years

Preschoolers possess a seemingly limitless energy. They explore their social and physical environments, testing limits and overcoming barriers with an unbridled spirit that challenges the equilibrium of the most giving and committed parent. "Looking back, I just don't know how I did it," commented a mother of four whose youngest child is now nine. "I just don't have that kind of energy anymore." "It's easy to see why God gave children to the young," one grandfather sighed after spending a long and hectic day following the trail of his three-year-old grandson.

During the preschool years, parents gain an increased knowledge and understanding of the characters and personalities of their children. Youngsters who, during infancy, seemed at least in part to be an extension of their parents, emerge as strong individuals with powerfully held desires and opinions.

A NEW PRESENCE IN THE HOME: COPING WITH THE GROWING INDEPENDENCE OF PRESCHOOLERS

Parents alternately describe the preschool years as invigorating, magical, exciting, frustrating, and overwhelming. On the positive side, they comment on the pleasure they gain from their children's perspectives on the world, since youngsters bring an untrammeled creativity to their interpretation of what goes on around them. Parents note and enjoy, for instance, the development of their child's sense of humor. "I can tell already he's going to have a good sense of humor. He enjoys good cartoons. He doesn't make jokes yet, but he plays with words and he enjoys puns," said one father. There is so much change during the years from two to five that parents are constantly surprised by what their children are up to. There is truth to the saying that children of this age literally grow before your very eyes. To the delight of their parents, they also become more sociable and affable, more companions and friends. "I like spending time with her now," remarked the mother of a four-year-old. "There is so much we can do together, and she can talk about so much more now. It's just fun to be together." Fathers, too, get a kick out of their preschoolers' new competence. It is now that children begin asking questions about their world, playing games, and weaving what can be elaborate fantasies. Children themselves get such pleasure from their newfound maturity that their enthusiasm is contagious.

On the negative side, however, the preschool years

can be fraught with difficulties for parents, some new
and some old. Despite their substantial gains, preschoolers still require constant adult supervision and
attention. They are dependent on their parents, not
only to meet their basic needs but to provide a secure,
nurturant base from which they can explore their
world. The preschool years are a period of testing and
exploration. Children are dependent on their parents
to provide safe limits within which they can express
their emotions and individuality, learn to deal with
others, and exercise their intelligence. They learn to
separate themselves from their parents. Preschool children continually ask their parents, either tacitly or
explicitly, "Is it safe to do this?" "How should I react?" "How far can I explore?" "Will you be here for
me when I get back?" The preschool years are marked
by a seemingly continuous need for self-assertion and
for discovering "Who am I?" and "How am I different
from you?" From the tantrums of a two-year-old trying
to get her own way to the stubbornness of a four-year-
old deciding what he wants to do next, preschoolers try
to carve a place for themselves. At almost every decision point, they look to their parents to take a stand.
Parents must learn to express their values in simple,
easily understood terms and to set reasonable limits on
how much room to allow for personal expression. They
must set standards regarding how much and in what
ways they expect their preschoolers to be responsible
and mannerly to other people. And they must draw the
line between acceptable and safe experimentation, on
the one hand, and potential danger and unacceptable
behavior, on the other.

During the preschool years, parents must establish

moral, emotional, and physical limits; they must also help interpret reality for their children. All parents of preschoolers have had the experience of watching their child fall down and scrape a knee or bruise a hand and then look to them as if to say, Does this really hurt? Is this something I should worry or complain about? Or should I forget about it and go on with my play? Similarly, preschoolers look to their parents to help them interpret their feelings, whether another child's action should make them angry or happy, whether a joke is hurtful or enjoyable.

Because preschoolers so continuously question their parents, life with preschoolers illuminates how many everyday decisions are governed by one's values. Whether or not parents feel they should allow their children to jump on the sofa, to scream when frustrated, or to hit back in a quarrel with another child— all these are reflections of the values parents hold and what they want their children to be like as adults. Mothers and fathers not only need to respond as individuals to the demands of their preschoolers for limits, they must agree as a couple on the values they present. They must work toward developing a mutually acceptable style of child rearing and discipline.

Mothers and fathers find that even discussions about seemingly trivial issues—such as when children are old enough to clean up their messy rooms—are based on more fundamental beliefs about the nature of family life and the responsibilities of children in the home. For instance, one mother, talking about whether children should bring their toys into the living room, summarized a discussion she had with her husband. "He says, 'It's all right if our house is messy. Children have to live here too.' And he's right. I keep reminding myself this is their house too."

Sometimes the fact that most decisions are based on fundamental values is forgotten in the midst of the hasty negotiations that must occur between two parents. It is common for parents to feel that they are caught in discussions that are trivial, if not ridiculous. For example, one mother described this appeal to her husband:

"When Mary was just about a year old, she toddled over to the trash can in the kitchen and started to pull out a handful of garbage. 'No,' I said. 'Don't play with the garbage.' She fixed me with this determined expression she uses when she is trying to figure out what I mean. First, she approached the garbage. Would I say no? Then she ever-so-gently stroked the side and then the lid of the garbage can and looked at me again. She lifted up the lid of the can and just peeked in. I found myself turning to my husband to ask, 'How would you define playing with the garbage?' "

The necessity to take a stand on everyday issues places parents' values under close scrutiny. If parents are not sure of their own values, or if, as a couple, they are in disagreement, their uncertainties and inconsistencies become apparent, both to their child and to themselves. Preschool children continually pressure their parents to agree on and confirm their standards. Both in order to enjoy parenting and to adequately present a united front to their children, mothers and fathers need to negotiate carefully and adapt their parenting styles to fit each other's. One couple we spoke with described how they had to develop their parenting style.

MOTHER: When they were little I would be with them from seven o'clock in the morning until sometimes seven or eight at night. By the time my husband came home I would be exhausted, and I wanted him to take over. Then, when he came in the door, I was no longer a parent.

FATHER: I just took over with the kids as soon as I got in from work. But sometimes, what would happen was when Daddy came home [I heard her say], "We're going to have to talk to Daddy about this."

MOTHER: I still do that.

FATHER: Not like you used to. It was bad, you know. I felt like the bad guy coming home, [as if I were] just there to dish out discipline. But we can't have that. You've got to do it right then and there.

In addition to confronting their own individual uncertainties and the differences that frequently emerge, parents must also come face-to-face with the reflection of their own parents in themselves. It is almost impossible to be a parent without thinking about and reacting to the way one's own parents acted. The way you were brought up yourself serves as a model— sometimes a positive one to be emulated, sometimes a negative one to be avoided—for how you will bring up your own child. In thinking about the parenting they themselves received, parents confront both the joys and sorrows of their own childhoods and of their relationships with their parents. Their reactions are as varied as their memories. One mother hopes she can be as good a mother as her own. Another, remembering with pain how stifled her mother always made her feel, hopes to do things differently with her own daughter. A father recalls the good times he had with his father, taking a walk, playing ball, and doing chores around the house, and resents his job, which prevents him from having the time to share the same experiences with his own children. Another man wants his children to know he cares deeply about them, a feeling he never received from his own father.

Regardless of their feelings about the parenting they received, under the relentless pressure of a preschooler's search for safe limits and answers to hard questions, parents often find themselves falling into the ways of their own parents. As one mother commented, "Without even thinking about it, I find myself reacting just like my mother did." For those mothers and fathers with admiration for their parents' style of raising children, the ability to dredge up their parents' reactions can be a wonderful and unexpected bonus. For others, though, the sense of redoing what they see as the serious mistakes of their own parents can be devastating. They feel they must work extra hard to strip themselves of the bad habits they learned while they were being parented.

Responsibility for preschoolers initiates parents into the complexities of assuming responsibility for another individual, one who is at once highly dependent and struggling for ever-increasing independence. In confronting the individuality of our preschool children, we must come to terms with our images of ourselves, of our own parents, and of what we want for our children.

NEW ARRANGEMENTS AND DECISIONS: EMPLOYMENT AND CHILD CARE

As children grow, mothers and fathers think and rethink the decisions about employment they made during their children's infancy. More and more mothers consider the possibility of working outside the home. Although currently half the nation's mothers of preschoolers remain out of the labor force, the other half are employed, some working part-time hours or for part of the year, the rest holding down full-time jobs. Mothers with preschoolers comprise the fastest growing contingent of the paid labor force. In 1950, just over 10 percent of married mothers with preschoolers were employed outside the home, including over 40 percent of those mothers without husbands. In 1980, well over 40 percent of all married mothers with children under five were in the labor force, as were almost 60 percent of unmarried mothers. Demographers have called this increase in maternal employment the most dramatic and significant social trend since the Second World War. Unlike most of their own mothers, the majority of mothers of preschoolers today, whether they are employed or not, have thought about the possibility of taking an outside job.

Mothers weigh the personal advantages of having a job and the extra income they can earn for their families against the advantages of staying home. Important as the new and expanding opportunities for women are, they create many dilemmas. After spending some time at home (even if it is just a few months), mothers ask themselves, "When is the right time to go back to work? Is there ever a perfect time?" Conversely, employed mothers find themselves wondering, "Am I missing out on too much because of my job? Would we all be better off if I didn't work right now?"

If they turn to experts to help them find the answers to these difficult questions, parents often come away more confused than ever. The experts simply don't agree. Some have advised mothers to stay home; they feel that young children need a parent's constant presence. Others report that employment of some kind is beneficial, not only to women but to their families. Daughters, in particular, are seen as gaining from watching their mothers successfully combine employment and child rearing.

In the light of the heated disagreements among professionals, it is not surprising that women also express a range of opinions about the benefits and costs borne by working mothers and their families. There are those who still believe that a woman's place is at home with her young children. "Children need their mothers at home. Why bother even having children if you don't want to stay home to raise them?" said one woman, and her sentiments are shared by many others like her. Others find that employment gives them stimulation and rewards that benefit their entire family. "When I go out into the world each day, I know more; I have experienced more; I am more of a whole person, and I can give more to my family." Still other mothers find their income essential to their family— either because there is no other earner or because their husband's income is low. To them, "Being a good mother *means* earning a living."

In an increasing number of families, in fact, maintaining the family standard of living requires the income that can be generated by a mother's employment. Only with the income from her job is the family able to afford the goods and services it deems necessary to support an acceptable quality of life. Furthermore, for an increasing number of mothers, work is a release from the constraints of home life, an opportunity to build a separate identity and focus of activities apart from the family. Employment is also protection against the possible exigencies of an unknown future.

Decisions about whether and where a mother should work as well as about the extent and nature of her employment are inextricably linked to parents' philosophies regarding the appropriate kind of child care for their preschooler. The decisions parents reach reflect how they weigh the relative significance of the quality of time they can spend with their youngsters against the quantity of time they feel they should spend at home. Is it the amount of time or the quality of time parents spend with their children that is of paramount importance? Scholars of child development and parents themselves disagree on the "right" answer. Yet parents must wrestle with this question as they figure out their work arrangements: To what extent do they need to be available to their children, and to what extent can they plan their time so as to be sure to include intensive interaction and enjoyable play, whether they are employed or not? There are few perfect solutions; it is mostly a matter of recognizing personal needs, values, and personalities and arriving at a comfortable arrangement. Women who choose to get a job are usually satisfied by how things work out and how well their family copes. Women who choose to stay home for a while longer are also generally pleased with their arrangements. It is women who don't have a choice—who are working only because they have to or who are home against their will—who have the most difficulty.

At times, parents feel hampered in arriving at good answers to the questions children raise because of the doubts, pains, and guilt that often accompany parenting. Preschool children are old enough to be away from parents for at least some of the time, yet often they are hurt or go through hard times as they experiment with their growing independence. They may fall down; they may have their feelings hurt by an angry friend; they may cry when their parents leave them with a baby-sitter or in a day-care center and then turn around and reject them when they return. It is difficult for parents to witness the trials of their preschoolers. It is equally difficult, if not more so, for parents to know their youngsters have experienced trouble in their absence.

Parents' reactions to the pains and anxieties of their preschool children reflect their own doubts about what constitutes adequate parenting. They also reflect parents' doubts about child rearing in an "unresponsive" society. If society is indifferent or even dangerous to young children, then a parent's responsibilities to protect a child are starker and more pressing. However, no matter how protective a parent may feel, it is clear that children need occasions to grow away from their parents and parents need occasions to be apart from their children. As parents debate the possibilities of maternal employment, they weigh their responsibility to protect children against their responsibility to provide them with new experiences and a range of opportunities.

Parents' decisions about whether to work and how to select the appropriate type of child care reflect the judgments they make of the wider society as a context for raising young children and the degree of protection and closeness to the family circle they deem necessary for children's safety and healthy development. In spite of the continuing debate about whether, when, and how much mothers should work, it is clear to scholars that the fact of employment does not represent any lessening in the commitment of mothers (or fathers) to provide good care for their children.

Women's employment choices are thus tied to the kind of child care parents feel is best. Decisions about child care, like most other decisions about preschoolers, reflect basic family values. Some parents believe that only family members are good for children. They speak eloquently about how children need to be cared for by those who love them best. Other parents believe that even young children can benefit from experiences with peers and other adults but that, even if children spend some time away from home, parents should remain their primary caretakers. Such parents might well both be employed, but they develop family work schedules that allow mother and father to share most of the parenting between them. Their child might attend a nursery program or a play group a few hours each day and then come home to be cared for by Father for part of the day and Mother the rest of the time. Parents might work split shifts, one leaving for work when the other arrives home, to provide such care. Still other parents wish their children to be exposed to stimulating environments and to professionals who are trained in child development and can introduce their youngsters to learning experiences not generally available at home. These parents might select a professionally staffed and well-run day-care center. The pragmatic arrangements parents make for the care of children are, at the core, an expression of the fundamental values they hold about the role mothers and fathers should play in child rearing.

Just as parents' values differ, so do their selections of child-care options. In families where mothers are employed full time, about 30 percent of children under six years old are cared for in their own homes: approximately 11 percent of these children are watched by their fathers, another 11 percent by a relative, such as a grandmother or an aunt, and 7 percent by some other unrelated individual. About half of all children whose mothers are working full time are cared for in someone else's home: they are taken to a relative, neighbor, or friend or to a family day-care home. Only about 15 percent of these children are cared for in group day-care centers. Interestingly, some children (about 8 percent) are cared for by their mothers while the mothers are working. When mothers are employed part time, their children are more likely to be cared for in their own home and less likely to be placed in a group care center.

The younger the children involved, the more likely they are to be cared for in a home, either their own or that of another. These statistics indicate that most parents continue to rely on homes and families for most of their child care. They see such arrangements as being the most nurturant (and affordable) alternatives for caring for preschoolers. Yet there is little evidence that quality group care harms children, that it detracts from their short-term happiness and well-being or their long-term development. Mothers employed full time may require the regularity of a day-care center, where such contingencies as illness or family problems do not interfere with the availability of care. Furthermore, mothers employed full time are also more likely to be able to afford the higher costs of good center care.

Mothers returning to work while their children are young weigh the advantages and strains of full-time employment against the relative ease of working part time. They think about the advantages of reliable, consistent, center-based child care and the advantages of warm, homelike family care. They consider what they want for themselves and for their children, and what their spouse wants and expects from them. The final selections families make reflect their values, their resources, and the willingness of husbands and wives to contribute both to the work of child care and to the work of providing the family income.

COMMUNITY SUPPORTS FOR PARENTING

Not only must parents present their personal values to their preschoolers and make life decisions that affect the well-being of their families, they must also begin wrestling with the larger social context in which their children will grow up. Mothers and fathers are often fearful of the society in which they are raising their children and uncertain of the standards they must maintain in a potentially dangerous social environment such as ours.

Preschoolers do not just query their parents about relatively uncomplicated issues of manners and play. They are also surprisingly aware of larger social issues, and their questions on these subjects force parents to confront their own uncertainties about the society they share with their children. Preschoolers don't limit their concerns to whether they can play with the garbage. They are curious about birth and death, sex, love and loneliness, and being good and being bad. One mother commented on her revulsion when her child casually reported the precautions suggested by her nursery school teacher to ensure that the child's Halloween candy would be safe: "I know she needs to be protected, but I hate the notion that she feels someone in our neighborhood might actually hurt her on purpose." Another mother recounted how confused she felt when her three-year-old daughter, having accidentally been allowed to see the end of a news clip showing the results of a recent massacre, came to her. "She asked me, 'Mommy, are those dead babies there? Who killed them? Would they kill me?' I didn't know how to answer her, how to be both honest and reassuring. How can you be reassuring to your children in today's world?"

Even very young children ask questions that lead to considerable soul-searching on the part of their parents. Mothers and fathers at times feel incapable of honestly projecting faith and trust to their preschoolers while still instilling in them the need to take reasonable precautions. Often, parents need the support of others. They need assistance in replying to the different moral questions posed by children. They need a means of providing their preschoolers with faith and hope in a world that is frequently threatening and unsafe.

It is not just that parents need the support of other parents in facing the daily strains of raising preschool children. Parents also recognize that their children are affected and endangered by events no one or two parents can change alone. Only in activities with other parents can any one family begin to have an impact on the issues of terrorism, anonymous crime in the community, and the worldwide threat of violence.

One public policy analyst has recently written a book entitled *Parenting in an Unresponsive Society*. In it she expresses one of the principal dilemmas faced by parents today. Our society, in its public policies, in its advice to parents, and in the services it provides to families, has not been particularly responsive to the needs of preschoolers or their parents. As a result, parents often feel unsupported and isolated. Our society offers parents few concrete supports even in providing basic public health services, such as inoculations, readily available well-baby checkups, or support when children require demanding twenty-four-hour nursing care.

As a further pressure, parents of preschoolers find that the larger society, while unresponsive to their needs, provides parents with what is often an unrealistic, even contradictory, model of what constitutes good parenting. Experts bombard parents with the best ways to clean, dress, feed, talk to, and play with their children. As a result, parents must learn to weigh advice and set limits on how much they let the experts dictate their actions. They must take care to remain spontaneous in their play, discipline, and interactions with their sons and daughters and to remain true to their own values and standards.

Even with help that they trust, however, many parents are aware of changes which seem to make their parenting goals almost obsolete. "My parents just wanted for us to be happy. I hope I can be the mother mine was, do for my family what she did. I'm trying to raise my children like I was raised. But the children today seem so much smarter. . . . They're supposed to be the same from generation to generation, but I find them very much smarter." Many parents worry that their children are "smarter"—they know too much too young. They are forced to be sophisticated beyond their years. All too often parents must raise their preschoolers, make decisions about jobs and careers, and work out their relationships with each other and with their neighbors and friends against a backdrop of a confusing, seemingly dangerous, and often unresponsive society.

One way for parents to surmount the pressures of parenting in our complex and often-isolating society is to turn to other parents for support. The social relationships developed by preschoolers themselves provide adults with the opportunity to forge new social networks. The parents of their child's nursery school classmates, the families of other children attending the same church, the parents of children living nearby, other parents at work: all can and often do become a supportive community of peers.

CHAPTER 4

The School Years: Sending Your Child Out Into the World

A child's entrance into school is a major landmark for parents. With the school years, both parents and children become increasingly engaged in a variety of community-based institutions and organizations that share some of the burden of educating and rearing our youngsters. Certainly the schools are the most prominent of those institutions serving children and families. Yet as they enter elementary school, many children also become more active participants in their churches; they begin to attend religious classes and services on a more regular basis. In addition, most communities offer an array of special services and programs that attract boys and girls, from Little League and soccer teams to Scouts and the local YMCA and YWCA or Boys Club. Since many of these groups (for example, the Scouts) solicit, or even require, mothers and fathers to participate along with their children, parents often find themselves drawn into new involvements during this stage of their lives. Typically, families with school-age children are among the most active members of their neighborhoods and towns.

As children participate in more activities outside the home, they meet many more children. They begin to form peer groups. It can be rewarding to watch children develop intimate friendships; it is satisfying to see children who have been loved and cared for by their parents learn how to care and express concern for others. But friends can also influence children's behavior and attitudes in ways that can seem unpredictable, undesirable, and even frightening to parents. In the course of their forays into the world, youngsters meet other children from different kinds of families, families with different value systems and different manners. The more that children are exposed to outside influences, the more that parents may see and hear things they *know* they never showed their youngsters. They may disapprove of the new language, jokes, games, hairstyles, and so on that enter their home. Children use their families to experiment with new ways of doing things and with behaviors they have learned in other settings and from other children. They evaluate the worth and appropriateness of these different styles, at least in part, by the reactions of their parents.

The school years are a busy time. Children are eager to learn more about the world they live in; they are curious and adventurous explorers. They want to learn what they can do and what they do best. They want to become competent and productive, and they are willing to work hard at developing new skills. They want guidance from their parents and teachers, and they are willing to listen to instructions and advice. But they also want the freedom to find out more about how their world works and what they can do for themselves.

Parents must provide an opportunity for children to meet new people and discover new things at the same time that they establish guidelines for safe and moral conduct. Most mothers and fathers enjoy this stage of their children's lives. Children are reasonable and adaptable; they develop their own interests and personalities. They are "little people" adventuring out into the world.

SENDING CHILDREN TO SCHOOL

Even though many children attend some form of preschool program, most parents look forward to the first day of elementary school with a mixture of anticipation and apprehension. Preschools are typically informal, small settings in which children are not formally evaluated or tested. Elementary school is different. The elementary school is an institution not only over which parents have relatively little control but also one which evaluates their offspring and, by extension, the job they themselves have done as parents. Whereas during the preschool years parents must come to terms with the growing individuality and independence of their youngsters, the school years are marked by a major new step. Parents must now subject these uniquely individual personalities who are their children to school, where, for better or worse, they will be expected to live up to our society's standards and expectations.

Certainly, many of the issues that emerge during the preschool years remain salient throughout the years of child rearing. Children continue to look to their parents for limits to their behavior, for guidance in interpreting their world, and for support when they are having a hard time. However, the school years are different from what comes before. Parents come to realize that their children, as they go out of the home, will need to exercise their values independently. Just teaching children skills and values is never enough; children need the opportunity to exercise their own judgment in contexts removed from the family. As one father commented, "The elementary [school] years are important—that's when children get their habits and their way of living." It is at this time that other institutions besides the family begin to have an impact on children, on their values and on their behavior.

Parents' concerns about what their children are exposed to in the classroom have increased over the last few decades primarily because of what many perceive as the steady decline in the quality of public education. What parent doesn't react to the frequent news reports about children who are roughed up by other children at school, about the lack of respect shown to teachers, and about the failure of schools to teach all children the skills they need for later life? Parents today not only feel a natural sense of loss and unease as their children move out of the home and into the wider society, they also fear what the schools are becoming and how children will be affected by their experiences.

In the United States, the schools are second only to the family as the institution in which children spend most of their waking hours. The public education system—originally established to create a literate citizenry—is charged now with a large number of additional tasks and functions. Schools typically are expected not only to teach the skills of literacy but also to introduce music and the arts and to prepare students to select among future jobs and educational opportunities. In many communities, schools also undertake sex education as well as education on morality and values and other ethical questions. In addition, they oversee basic public health for children by enforcing regular checkups and inoculations and by screening for a variety of health problems to which children are vulnerable. They also may provide counseling and mental health services to children and to their families.

Because schools perform so many functions in the lives of children, they at times end up in an adversarial stance against parents on issues more or less related to strictly educational concerns. Some parents feel that schools are not concentrating sufficiently on the basic skills of literacy; they are concerned that schools rather than families are handling such issues as sex or moral education. Still other parents feel that schools reflect a political stance contrary to their own. Such parents may feel that schools are infringing on the duties and responsibilities of the family. As one parent commented:

"I really feel like one of the things we've done is put this incredible load on the schools and that there're certain times we want them to be parent figures and other times we don't. It's got to drive the schools crazy. As a parent I want it real clear as to what the school's role is with my child, and what my responsibilities are. I guess I don't like all the parental responsibilities that I see being placed on the schools. I want them myself. I hear things like there are classes now in ethics and morality and things like that. . . . I don't like the way I

see a lot of people sitting around arguing ethics. I
disagree with it very strongly, especially institution-
alized ethics and morality, which you're going to get in
the school. I definitely want the responsibility as a
parent to instill that. . . .

"I don't mind a school teaching my child to question. I think that's very appropriate. To question what's
moral and what's not. But I don't want them providing
their answers. That's where I draw the line. I think the
school's role is to teach my child to think for himself,
not to give him answers to those sorts of issues."

Even when parents consider their community
schools as relatively benevolent institutions, they can
feel they don't have the control they want over what
happens in the classroom. Parents doubt the possibility of their impact on the schools for a variety of
reasons.

First, the state of public schools reflects the condition of the economy. When times are hard, not only
families but the institutions that serve them are affected. Schools and classes get larger. Materials and
teachers specializing in special topics are spread thin-
ner. Services for children with special physical or
educational needs are limited. The school functions on
which parents have learned to depend may be elimi-
nated.

Also, because schools reflect community politics and
norms, because they reflect the regulations of the fed-
eral government, and because they reflect the state of
the national and local economy, schools may be unresponsive to the specific needs of individual families.
Parents often express their concern that schools en-
courage competition rather than cooperation, that they

are ill equipped to serve children who are not bright, eager, and free of any learning difficulties; that they take too little account of the differing backgrounds of children and the interests and expectations of different parents. Schools often seem to be an expression of majority mores. Parents who are members of racial or ethnic communities, of other language groups, or of religious minorities may feel that the schools to which they send their children do not inculcate the culture, values, and skills they wish their children to have.

Yet parents have realized that they are not powerless with regard to the schools. There are many ways parents can and do become involved with their children's education. They vote in local elections for school board members of their choice and on issues of relevance to the schools, such as the local tax base; they serve on school boards and special committees; they participate in the PTA and other parent organizations; they volunteer time in the classroom; they make it a point to be available for class trips and special events; they attend teacher conferences and school nights; they organize fund raisers to raise money for special equipment and programs.

Because of their employment patterns, it is typically mothers, rather than fathers, who keep a careful eye on what is going on at school. Many like to spend some time as school volunteers, since such work gives them the opportunity to see their children's teachers in action. Parents also report that children like to see them involved and interested. As one mother explained, "I think there comes a stage and age when they don't want you in things with them. But right now, if there's a field trip or whatever, my kids want me to be on it. They like seeing me there; they like knowing I care about what's going on." By participating in the schools, parents gain knowledge about the conditions of their community schools, about the quality of the teachers, and about what's taught and what's not. They can then use this information and the contacts they have made to try to change what they don't like and to get the best possible education for their children. Because of the importance of parental participation and mothers' and fathers' awareness of the need to keep in close contact with the schools, PTA membership and school-related volunteering are the most common forms of community participation by adults at this stage in the family cycle.

Despite their acknowledgment of some difficult problems, most parents stick with the public schools because they have a fundamental belief in the principle of public education. They believe that society at large is responsible for providing an education to all children, and they believe that their children should participate in the major democratic institution available to them. Furthermore, they feel that only by participating through their children's enrollment and their own involvement in public schools can parents contribute to activities that lead to the maintenance and improvement of public education in their communities. However, for some parents, private and parochial schools offer attractive possibilities. They tend to be more homogeneous, and children are likely to meet children from other families who share their own fundamental values and notions about education. Through the private and parochial schools, parents are offered a selection of educational programs and programs dealing with ethical and religious issues. Particularly for parents in communities with a faltering public education system, decisions about which school to use and how much parental involvement the family can afford to contribute are difficult ones.

Often, though, there is little choice. Unless parents have considerable financial resources, it is not necessarily a realistic solution simply to change schools. To do so, they either have to uproot their families and move so they can use the public schools of another community or they have to purchase the often expensive services of a private or parochial school. Some families can afford to do this. Most, however, decide that their only alternative is to work with the school most readily available to them.

Because parents may disagree with some school policies and practices, they may be uncertain about how to talk to their children about the schools as institutions and the education they receive. It is traditional lore that parents should support the teachers of their children, enforcing similar rules at home, encouraging the completion of school assignments, and backing the teacher's authority in the classroom. However, when parents find themselves in disagreement with the schools or with the individual teacher of their child, they may feel torn between their duty to the schools as the tool of their child's education and their need to reflect their own values and beliefs to their children.

Thus, as children enter school, parents often find themselves compelled to become involved in the local politics that control schools and in the parent groups through which individuals can work both to enrich

educational programs and to influence school admin-
istrations. Difficult though schools may be to change,
parents find that they can and do have a considerable
effect on what is taught, how it is taught, and what
special programs are made available to children.

For many adults, the fact that political and group
activity can be an important part of parenting is a new
concept. Yet, through this kind of involvement, parents are likely to have the greatest chance of affecting
the schools their children attend. Parents comment on
their responsibility to attend PTA meetings and express their anxiety if the pressures of work or the needs
of other children in the family prevent them from
being as active in the schools as they want to be.

In spite of the problems and the deep concerns
generated by the perceived condition of public education in this country, parents in general remain committed to public education. They point with pride to
new programs and to the achievements of students in
their schools. They take great pride in their own
children's school accomplishments. They enjoy their
children's growing skills and the competence that al-
lows their children to learn and grow in the larger
institution of the school. One mother reflected, "I
enjoy them coming home from school and the work
that they've done and their pride in their work. And I
enjoy helping them with their homework once in a
while. And if they're chosen for things at school, it
makes me proud."

CHURCHES AND OTHER INSTITUTIONS
AFFECTING CHILDREN

Important as the schools are, they are not the only institution to affect children's education and development during the school years. Many families turn to formal religious organizations for support as they try to instill faith and a firm sense of moral beliefs in their children. Responsibility for school-age children often revives in parents a need for church involvement that they did not feel during their young adult and childless years. As one father commented, "I've never been much of a joiner, and I stopped going to church as soon as I stopped living with my parents. But now that I have a child, I feel our family needs a church to help us give our children a sense of right and wrong. We need to meet other people who are trying to do the same thing. I suspect in the next few months we will begin attending the church down the street pretty regularly."

In ways similar to how parents seek out others for support in facing the questions raised by the public schools, parents also seek out other families in the context of a religious organization that can support them as they present religious and ethical values to their children. Churches can become a partner with parents in expressing important values to children. Parents look to churches to express and demonstrate important beliefs and they depend on their church to mirror in large part their own values. In times of stress and when facing complex problems, parents may turn with their children to their church for a consistent statement of the applicable moral laws and values.

Church is a more personal institution than is the school in several important ways. Membership in a congregation directly reflects a combination of an individual's upbringing and personal choice. Unlike school attendance, church membership is not mandatory. Although other families and the community at large can bring considerable pressure to bear on an individual, in the end a person's involvement in the church is a reflection of his or her own decision.

However, as is the case with schools, parents need to be active agents rather than passive attenders to gain the most benefits for their families. Churches provide many activities and services besides formal religious observances, and in almost all churches these activities are supported by the volunteer labor of the congregation. Parents' groups, children's groups, and service work in the larger community all require the involvement of church members. In addition, the fact that churches can be supportive does not mean that disagreements and differences between families and religious institutions never arise. Just as parents are called on to explain the values of the church to their children, they are at times forced to explain the differences and lapses that occur between the theology and behavior proposed by the church and the realities and pressures of family life. As children grow older and more sophisticated, they try to understand the differences among the value systems to which they are exposed. They want to understand just where their parents stand. They question them on any perceived lapse from expressed values.

The expression and teaching of values does not depend on church membership, of course, and many families are not active in a church. It is the rare family, however, that does not become involved in some type of organization because of the interests and needs of their children. Youngsters lead their parents to a variety of other institutions in the community besides the schools and churches. School-age children attend many recreational and educational programs, including scouting organizations, sports teams and clubs, tutoring programs, Y's, and a great many others. These activities—primarily designed to serve children—make many of the same demands on parents as do churches and schools. First, many are staffed, at least in part, by volunteer parents. Parents as well as children become part of the organization, contributing to it at the same time as they receive benefits for their families. Such participation provides the pragmatic support required by these organizations to function; it also represents a statement to children that these activities are important and valuable enough to draw in parents too.

Peripheral though these organizations may at times appear, participation in them provides additional messages to children of important values in the community and family. They help teach children the importance of civic participation. Whether the emphasis is on education, art, music, service activities, athletic skills, or learning to compete or simply on the skills of getting along with others, these extracurricular involvements can be extremely beneficial to children. The devotion of family resources to these programs reflects parental values about the importance of such activities and community participation.

Thus the school years are a time when parents add to their at-home responsibilities the job of overseeing and becoming involved in those institutions that serve their children. Schools, churches, and the other organizations in which children are engaged instill values and beliefs. Of course, parents remain the primary figures in their children's lives, but as children grow older, they become increasingly affected by their relationships in the wider community. Insofar as the aims of local institutions are at variance with parental beliefs, parents may find themselves working to effect change. However, where institutions do reflect important family values, they can provide immense support to parents who are under pressure, even when they require contributions of parental time and effort in return.

CHILDREN'S FRIENDS AND PEER GROUPS

Becoming active in political and other organizational activities is not the only way parents can mediate the impact of schools and other organizations on their children. These institutions do not only affect children through their administrative structure and ties to the norms of the community. They also affect children by providing large peer groups of other children, which have a significant impact on how children behave, on the values and moral stands they assume, and on their relationship with their parents.

The exposure of children to others from different kinds of families with different values is, of course, stimulating and important. But involvement with other children can and does present problems to parents. Learning from their peers, children may express values contrary to those in which their parents believe. They may wish to undertake activities that parents consider either dangerous or wrong. They may wish to indulge in luxuries which involve considerable time, effort, or expense and which seem relatively unimportant to their parents.

School children confront their parents with the well-known phrase "But everybody does it." Parents hear this immortal statement regarding issues ranging from having one's ears pierced to spending all day Saturday at the local shopping mall to playing video games to skipping school for a special movie to whether it's the right time to start dating. Because most communities include families with a range of standards, parents frequently must decide how questions raised by their child relate to fundamental family values. Is this a time for "Our family is simply different, and we don't do this"? Or is this a time when parents can bend to allow their child to be like other children? Parents feel the need to teach children to make their own judgments. "I try to tell my daughter, Please, have a mind of your own. To know right from wrong. And to try to do the right thing," reported one mother.

During the preschool years, children demanded limits and standards from their parents out of their need to understand and control themselves. During the school years, children continue to require limits and parental expressions of values. However, now they are dealing with a more complex environment; they are learning to weigh the opinions of both their parents and their peers against their own. Children still need to hear a strong message from their parents on what is important, but they are likely to make comparisons between what their parents think and what their friends think.

At times, children learn information from their peers that their parents might well wish to have protected them from. Children from homes where television-viewing is restricted are likely to learn of more adult shows from their friends as well as see such fare when they go visiting. Children from homes that prohibit playing with guns and games of violence will be exposed to them at school and often encouraged to play them when away from home. Children will experiment with language that parents consider unacceptable.

When children are exposed to frightening or dangerous alternatives outside the home, parents often feel at a loss as to how to teach and protect their children. One mother of four elementary school-age children commented, "My only hope, I think, is fear. It's a terrible thing, but I feel this way. It's like teaching a little child not to cross the street alone. If you cross the street, you're going to get hit by a car and killed. I try to tell them the same thing with drugs. Those kids who touch them, as soon as they touch them, they're dead. Their life is over, they're dead." The need some parents feel to inspire fear in their children is symptomatic of the degree of fear and apprehension that parents feel as their children start making their own way in the world. But together with these doubts is the parents' pride in seeing children become active and productive members of their communities. Sending children out into the world can be tough, but it can also be enormously rewarding as parents see their children acting on what they have learned at home.

PARENTS' RESPONSE TO THE SCHOOL YEARS

Husbands and wives turn to each other and to other parents for help in responding to the pressures of child rearing at this and every other stage of the family life cycle. They also think about their own life decisions and how they will affect their children: what kinds of jobs, what kinds of educational opportunities, what kinds of volunteer work they can assume now that their children are in school.

Parents, and mothers in particular, often foresee the school years as a time of increasing freedom. Children are out of the home a substantial portion of each day. By the time the children are in school, most parents believe they are old enough to visit their friends and even be away for occasional overnights. Older school-age children can even be left at home by themselves, at least for short periods of time.

Indeed, there is some relief from the pressures of parenting preschoolers. Mother can run across the street to borrow a cup of sugar from a neighbor or dash to the grocery store, leaving an older school-age child unattended. She is not tied to the home and child in the same way. She is likely to have somewhat more time to devote to herself and her own activities. As school-age children develop their own interests and friends, so can parents.

However, difficult issues remain for parents as they plan their own lives. As we have already explained, the more children become involved with other children and other institutions, the more parents are drawn to these institutions and the more they feel the need to spend at least some time devoted to such activities. Furthermore, because children are moving more freely through their neighborhoods, parents may be more fearful of the possible emergencies and accidents that might arise. They want to *be there* if their child falls off a bike, has a fight with friends, or is tearfully struggling with incomprehensible homework. They want to be available after school should their child need them.

This means that although many mothers are back in the paid labor force by the time their children are of school age, they may still be curtailing their employment, both in terms of hours they work and the type of job pressures they feel they can handle. Women work to earn as much as their family needs. They work to maintain their career. But their work involvement is still affected by their perceptions of their children's needs. The needs of school-age children are certainly different from the needs of preschool children. However, to their surprise, some parents find that they are more comfortable if one parent is home when children are not in school. They feel that children still need a parent at home at least part of the time.

For other parents, the school years seem a remarkably good time to return to a heavy investment in the labor force. The children are involved in outside activities, and the parents feel good about the programs to which they entrust their children's care. They take care to provide adequate supervision for their children during the afterschool hours while both parents are still at work.

The fact that more and more mothers are taking on heavier commitments to their jobs and careers during their children's school years has created a demand for a new kind of family service, school-age child care. Employed mothers need to know that their children will be well cared for even if both parents have to leave the home before the school day starts and do not return home until well after it is over.

The type of care and supervision required by school-age children varies widely according to the kind of community in which they live, the hours for which they need care, and the age of the child. In some communities, crowded with busy streets and troubled by a range of urban problems, parents may feel the need for close supervision after school, in a setting where adults can keep a close watch on the children's activities. In smaller communities, presenting fewer dangers, children may be allowed to range over the neighborhood on bike or on foot; they may require only the loose supervision of a "safe house" mother with whom they check in and to whom they can go in an emergency.

These services themselves are extremely important to employed parents of school-age children, and, like all services and organizations in which their children participate, they are likely to make demands on parents. Some programs are cooperatives demanding a time commitment. If parents wish to have some control over their children's environment, they at least must spend the time and energy necessary to discuss any issues and disagreements that arise with caregivers and administrators of the program.

As children grow older, it is natural for mothers and

fathers to think they will have more time and energy to devote to their jobs and to other activities that interest them. And indeed this is true. With the school years does come a new sense of freedom from the constraints of caring for preschoolers. But school-age children continue to need a parent's time and attention. They need to know their parents are interested and involved in their lives and activities. The demands of parenting change as children make their way through elementary school, but one thing remains constant. Through personal interaction with their offspring and through their involvements in schools, churches, and other child-serving organizations, parents remain their children's most important teachers.

CHAPTER 5

Adolescence: Launching the Young Adult

Most parents approach their children's adolescence with considerable dread. Parents of teenagers tell parents of younger children, "Just wait until they're teenagers. You don't know what problems really are yet." One mother, when asked to give advice on parenting teenagers, commented, "You just have to remember you are not talking to a rational human being, you're talking to raging hormones." During adolescence, the period of transition between childhood and adult status, parents watch the children they have nurtured for over a decade put into use the behaviors, skills, emotions, and values they have learned during their preschool and school years.

Parents experience pain as well as pride as they see their children gaining independence. Even as their teenagers continue to draw on families for strength, they may reject some long-standing values and traditions. The questioning and rejection of parents that is a normal part of every child's development is often difficult for mothers and fathers to understand or deal with. During their children's teenage years, parents themselves are likely to be in mid-life, a period when many adults start questioning their own values and the worth of their experiences and contributions. It is this blending of the life stage of teenagers and the life stage of parents that creates the experience of parenting teenagers.

TEEN PHOBIA

"Oh, I'm not looking forward to those days!" a mother of a five-year-old reported. "I think it's got to be one of the most difficult times. Looking back to my own adolescence, there are just so many ambivalent feelings. I guess that the parent has simply got to remain the older and wiser person and not get sucked into thinking either that their child is a grown person or that this kid is a completely dependent being. Children are testing and trying to figure out when they can be solidly independent and when they can't. Somebody in all that craziness has got to keep their wits about them. It's got to be the parent. ... The years from eight to twelve are supposed to go so smoothly. Everything's okay and then all of a sudden it's all crazy. You've got to get your sea legs as the parent of a teenager."

Parents of younger children jokingly propose solutions for dealing with the teenage years. "Send them all off to an island by themselves and then let them return when they're twenty," one parent suggested. Another proposed "a convent school for all seventh- and eighth-graders—that's *really* the worst time."

Newspaper accounts, self-help volumes for parents, and discussions with parents of teenagers all appear to substantiate this fear of the teenage years. Living with a teenager can be difficult; at times it can seem almost impossible. Remembering how they treated their own parents when they themselves were going through puberty makes even the most unflappable parent feel a little queasy. There is no use denying that these can be tough years: few would believe it. Yet sometimes the toughest times with children are also the most challenging and the most thought provoking.

Teenagers can be volatile, disrespectful, and un-predictable. Parents are often relatively powerless to control or even influence their activities. This lack of control can be the hardest thing for parents to accept. It is not just that they can't control whether their own son drinks and then goes driving; how can they make sure he never takes a ride with a friend who has had one too many for the road?

Parents' worries about the safety and well-being of their teenagers run the gamut from the abstract to the concrete, from concern with the society in which their children will have to form their future lives to fretting about the daily activities in which their children en-gage. Parents are anxious and uncertain about the nature of the world their children will face as adults. As one mother said, "I'm raising my children for a world I can hardly imagine. What will it be like in twenty years? Who knows. I can never know whether what I teach my girl will equip her for the challenges she will face. They will be challenges I can't even imagine right now."

As their children are maturing into young adults, parents are more likely to see the connection between national and international policy issues and their

family's future. Policies become more tangible; they
are ever more likely to affect their children. Job dis-
crimination hits home if a daughter cannot find a job
because she is female, or a son is unemployed because
he is black. U.S. involvement in foreign wars becomes
a more pressing family concern as sons approach draft
age. Of course some parents have been concerned
about these issues before their children reach adolescence. But society's problems are most likely to become personal and urgent as our children prepare to
launch themselves into the adult world. It can be
agonizing even to think about the children we love
suffering for the abstract policies we often feel we
cannot affect or dying for causes we do not support.

Parents are not solely concerned about the state of
the world and its effect on their children. They worry
too about the specific decisions their children will
make about jobs and careers, further schooling, sex,
drugs and drink, and where, how, and with whom to
set up housekeeping. One mother comments:

"Our son has just completed his first year of college.
He went to a military school because he wants to join
the Navy and become a naval navigator. Well, I wasn't
thrilled with his choice—I'd rather he wasn't in the
military—but at least he was making a choice and
planning. Now he comes home for the holidays. He got
a poor grade in a math course he expected to do well
in. He says he sees no point in continuing in school
when he can just enlist. The recruiter says he doesn't
have to go to college now. The Navy will train him. I
try to tell him not to make a life decision because of a
poor math grade. I try to tell him the Navy doesn't
assign people to jobs just because the people want

those jobs. But he doesn't seem to hear me, and it's his life. I can talk, but I can't stop him."

As children mature and start making their own life decisions, parents watch to see to what extent their youngsters have assimilated family values. Parents are sometimes caught off guard by the depth of their feelings when children turn away from the models the parents have presented. One mother, heavily invested in her career and proud of her progressive parenting, described her chagrin as she heard her daughter dismiss the possibility that she herself would have children. Hadn't the child seen how much parenting meant to the mother?

Perhaps most difficult of all, parents know their children have special and important worries of their own. Elizabeth Winship, who writes an advice column for teenagers called "Dear Beth" in *The Boston Globe*, has printed letters from teenagers reflecting their fears of the world they are growing up into. Here is one example:

Dear Beth,
    People say us kids have it easy, and that teenage is "the best years of your life." Well, I'm 13, and I don't feel so carefree and easy. The main thing I worry about is if I'll ever live to grow up. The idea of nuclear war scares me so much. I have dreams that our house is mashed flat, and we are all lying out in the street with our faces black and our hair burned off, like those pictures of people in Japan. How can we ever escape?
    If we do live long, there may not be any gas left, or even any food. The air may all be polluted, and we will die of cancer. My parents say it is foolish to worry, and they will take care of me, but I see the

news, and I can see what is going on. Sometimes I
wish I were a little baby again, and didn't have to
think about it.—Dumb Kid

Parents' images of the teenage years are colored by
their worries about the world into which they are
sending their children. Mothers and fathers are sometimes stymied by their doubts about whether they
have adequately equipped their children for an unknown future. They perceive that children today have
not only the age-old concerns about reaching maturity
but also an overlay of new and frightening issues to
confront, from dealing with the increases in personal
freedoms and expression to handling the prospect of
nuclear devastation.

The difficulties of this period are not made easier by
the type of experimentation in which many teenagers
choose (in some cases, need) to engage. Because this is
a period when children require considerable independence, their decisions are often unknown until
after the fact and may appear mystifying to parents.
Parents ask themselves how children raised with *their*
family values could possibly use language, adopt manners, try out drugs, or drink in the ways that they in fact
are doing. It is hard to understand why youngsters
suddenly appear uninterested in school, in family activities, or even in the recreation and creative activities that so engrossed them just a few years before.

It is not simply what adolescents are doing that can
dismay and mystify parents. It is also that the lines of
communication between parent and child seem to shut
down. Teenagers can be very difficult to talk to. As one

father summed up his experiences, "Teenagers are either withdrawn and miserable or angry, loud, and miserable." Even what seems to a parent like the smallest and most benign comment can elicit an extraordinarily powerful response from a teenager. "My daughter thinks I'm the most embarrassing individual in the world. If I say I like the outfit she's wearing, it's 'Mother, I wouldn't be caught dead outside the house in this. You're so conservative.' I hardly dare comment on something I don't like," explained one perplexed mother.

On top of all these struggles and problems, however, the truth is that teenagers are trying to act like independent adults who can be trusted to make reasonable, conscionable decisions. They are learning to stand up for themselves, to have the strength of their convictions, and to take responsibility for their own actions. These are difficult acts for adults as well as teenagers. Parents get pleasure from witnessing their teenagers' efforts even as they themselves suffer through the natural mistakes their teenagers will make. Teenagers are willing to take a stand and follow it through with conviction. They are willing to put up a fight for what they think is right and what they think they deserve. Their sense of righteousness, their energy, and their very youth can fill their parents with pride.

It is important for parents to remember that anxiety about the teen years of their children can become a self-fulfilling prophecy. All parents report some difficulties with their teenage children, but parents must step back from their immediate involvement with these problems to assess the real significance of the troubles they are having. Two mothers of different teenagers may use the same vocabulary and even strength of emotion to describe their problems: their adolescent child is "impossible," "damaging the family as well as himself," and "impossible to reach through any rational communication." However, one mother may be complaining because her son is often late for dinner; another because her son is experimenting with drugs.

Because we have been continually impressed with the difficulties of raising adolescents, it is easy to see all our problems with adolescents as enormous and overpowering. Parents of adolescents need to allow themselves the distance to realize that it's not the end of the world if their teenager is late for dinner. They may still remonstrate with the teenager about the tardiness, and they may still be concerned. In fact, they need to show their teenager that they notice and care. But they must also remind themselves that such action is neither inherently dangerous nor necessarily even disrespectful. Because of the times we live in and because of the extent of our "teen phobia," it is too easy for parents to magnify the difficulties, to overlook the satisfactions of seeing a child develop into an adult.

PARENTS' EMPLOYMENT
THROUGH THE TEENAGE YEARS

The teen years, like the school years, are a time many parents reassess their own life directions and decisions. They think about the efforts of the first two decades of their adult lives, they wonder whether they have made appropriate decisions, and they weigh the implications of their earlier choices. For some adults, this kind of personal reflection results in what has been labeled the "mid-life crisis." Both men and women are subject to some kind of mid-life crisis. However, because the life experiences of men and women during their twenties and thirties are usually so different, the issues that arise at this time are likely to be different for members of each sex.

Women, as we have discussed, are more apt to have put their jobs and careers on a back burner. Of course, many women have been employed during their children's preschool and school years. However, for the large majority of women, the extent of their investment in jobs, career advancement, and continuing education was contained as they concentrated on raising children and providing a comfortable home. As a result, many mothers look forward to their late thirties and forties, the typical time of their children's adolescence, as a period when they can become more involved in their work outside the home, can allow themselves to make more commitments, and can undertake the kinds of activities that would lead to their own personal development.

Furthermore, family expenses only seem to increase during this stage of the family cycle. Families now face the possible expenses of college education for their children, as well as the increasing costs of teenagers' clothes, recreation, and incidental school expenses. Even those relatively few mothers who till this time had not considered their income essential to the family are likely to see expenses looming that will require their earnings. Thus, as a result of both personal desire and family needs, mothers are likely to see this as a period when they will change their priorities and increase their commitments to activities away from the family sphere.

However, decisions about employment, returning to school, further involvement in volunteer activities, and other possibilities outside the homemaking realm are not necessarily as different and as free of child-rearing constraints as we might expect them to be as children get older. Many parents feel that their adolescents are very vulnerable, very much in need of adult contact and supervision. Children are exposed to temptations both at school and in their neighborhoods and peer groups. Like their parents before them, they face many temptations—drugs, sex, cars, alcohol. Because of their concern, parents continue to make decisions about their jobs and careers in the light of their assessment of the kind of time and involvement their children may require at home. They still worry about whether or not they should be at home when their children come home at the end of the school day. They don't want their children (and their children's friends) coming home to an empty house. They still make plans to be available to children who may experience a sudden crisis or emergency or who may just feel a sudden need to talk to their parents. The teen years may be difficult for parents in part because they are not quite as free of child-rearing responsibilities as they might have believed.

This can create a conflict, because personal freedom and the opportunity for self-development may be particularly important to women during the years when they are parenting adolescents. Women who have been mothering for ten or fifteen or twenty years often feel a strong urge to devote more time, energy, and family resources to their own needs for career, education, or just time to sit and contemplate new books and ideas. It can be difficult to realize that adolescents, although different from younger children, can still have a powerful impact on their mothers' lives and daily activities.

The teen years are likely to have a major impact on fathers, too. Fathers typically have been closely tied to their jobs during their children's preschool and school years. When they are raising young children, fathers are likely to feel strong pressures to earn the family living. "My first responsibility is to my family's livelihood: shelter, food, clothing, schools, the necessities. I can never make any decisions that jeopardize my ability to give them what they deserve," said one father.

However, in mid-life, some men find themselves depressed and unsatisfied as they think about their future employment. For men who have stayed tied to a particular job or occupation out of concern for the stability of family income, there comes a time when they wonder whether this is how they should have spent their energies. They may feel that in twenty or so years of hard work they haven't really accomplished all that much. Particularly if fathers feel that they are having problems with their teenage children, they may wonder whether they have followed the right course or whether they should try to change in midstream.

At times fathers feel that they have had little opportunity for experimentation. Because they have been wary of jeopardizing their job security, fathers may feel a sense of lost opportunities. Even though they may have devoted considerable effort to advancement on the job, increasing their earnings and gaining higher status and prestige, they may feel a sense of loss, of accomplishing less than they had expected.

If fathers have primarily devoted themselves to the job, they may find themselves feeling somewhat distanced from their children and family life. Fathers concerned with earning a living—and this can be true whether or not their wives are also employed—may feel they do not know their children as well as they wish. The formative, childhood years have somehow slipped by. Particularly when adolescents may be acting out their disagreements with parents, it may seem that their children are relative strangers. Fathers may look back at twenty years of devotion to the task of earning a living for these same children and feel a sense of discouragement and letdown.

Last, both mothers and fathers may feel a hard-to-recognize resentment of their teenage children. Parents questioning the values of their own lives and the possibility of future alternatives are continuously faced with the image of their young and relatively carefree children whose whole lives are in front of them. Much as parents love their teenage children and work for their future, it is hard to avoid the unsettling comparison between their own middle years and the youth of their children.

As is the case during the earlier years of parenting, mothers and fathers can help each other face mid-life issues. It is important to help each other recognize that this is a critical life stage, one with which many other parents are familiar. Because parents find themselves questioning their priorities and wondering about their life alternatives, it may seem to them that life has taken a downturn. But this period of questioning is a necessary prelude to the recognition that mid-life adults still have a lively future ahead of them, one that will be, within another four or five years, relatively unencumbered by children. Without the questioning and the reassessment, parents would be unable to take advantage of what amounts to a second chance. As their children are making their way into the world, parents too are making decisions and rethinking their priorities in ways that will affect their lives.

INSTITUTIONAL AND COMMUNITY TIES FOR PARENTS OF TEENAGERS

Just as parents may find themselves growing somewhat distant from their teenage children, so they may feel that they are separating from the services and organizations in which they spent time when the children were younger. The independence of children during their adolescent years brings with it the relative independence of parents from volunteering time to their children's activities. Certainly parents of teenagers continue to work with many child-serving organizations. But, in contrast to younger children, teenagers don't often want their parents around. They want some autonomy. In order to meet teenagers' requirements for independence, most high schools provide a range of programs to students and allow them to select from a variety of possible courses. Although in most systems parents must approve the choices of their children, it is also the case that few schools will insist on teenagers entering programs in which they themselves have no interest. Furthermore, beyond the formal educational curriculum itself, schools offer a number of possibilities to teenagers. Most high schools offer organized intramural and competitive sports. In spite of budget cuts, most offer a variety of other courses ranging from drama and music to chess and bridge to extracurricular computer and technical work. It is part of the design of these programs that teenage participants get to decide on the nature of their activities and help direct and lead the activity as well as participate and benefit from it. Clubs and extracurricular organizations have student presidents and organizers. Teams have captains. The student body itself is often organized with elected officers, who have control over certain school rules and disciplinary procedures, budget, and the authority to plan a variety of social and recreational functions.

Adolescents not only feel a strong need to take control over some of the institutions and organizations that control their lives. They often also feel a need to protect their newfound independence, by denying their parents active involvement and even by attempting to deny them information. Parents of teenagers may feel that they don't have much effect on the organizations run by their children; they often cannot even learn what is going on. Teenagers might reply "It's a secret" or just "Nothing much happens there" in response to parents' questions about activities.

For parents concerned with their children's future, this lack of communication can be particularly infuriating where it applies to events connected with the school and their children's education. When children appear to resent discussing their academic program with their parents and dislike involving their parents in their work, parents may feel denied the critical opportunity to help their children toward the necessary achievements for college, career, or other vocational opportunities. It can be difficult also to judge—with such limited information as teenagers often provide—whether a child is facing major problems in school or just the ordinary difficulties suffered by most adolescents.

Church youth groups, Scouts, and other social groups also expect that teenage participants will want and need the experience of taking responsibility for their own activities. Children at this age may require some adult participation and supervision, but they frequently prefer the adults *not* to be their own parents. They want the experience of dealing with others, of developing intimacy with nonfamily members. "They tell me everything," said one high school teacher, "things I'm sure they'd never tell their parents." In fact, when adolescents do not feel they have been granted opportunities to undertake the responsible management of the organizations that serve them, adults are sometimes surprised and dismayed to realize that the teenagers are likely to form their own much less innocuous secret clubs, sororities, and fraternities, over which they hold control by keeping them invisible to adult eyes.

As teenagers assume control over many of their activities, parents may find themselves in the position of compromising their own values. For instance, parents in many communities are surprised to discover that schools are planning all-night senior proms. Because students wish to stay out all night, schools have agreed with student organizations that it is better to have them out all night at an organized school function than in unsupervised cars or small groups. "I never thought I would ever be brought to allow my daughter to stay out all night on a date. But what can I do? The school is sponsoring this dance. And all her friends are going. It's hard to tell what's right," reported one parent.

Parents who have devoted so many years to their children may feel hurt by teenagers' demands to be left alone and by their refusal to continue to learn from their parents' experiences. It is easy to interpret the teenager's need for independence as rejection. It is easy to be suspicious of the teen's need for privacy. "Why does my child put three doors between the two of us before discussing a homework assignment with her best friend? What can they be talking about all the time that they don't want me to hear?" questioned the mother of a sixteen-year-old daughter. In the thick of the situation, it can be difficult to remember that a need for privacy and independence does not necessarily mean that teenagers are succumbing to dangerous temptations or are doing bad things. They may simply need to do things by themselves, without their parents looking on.

Because the organizations in which adolescents participate do not require the same kind of investment on the part of parents, parents are often not presented with the same opportunities for contact with other parents. Parents of adolescents are not naturally brought together to oversee social functions, plan the policies of groups in which their children participate, or closely supervise their activities. Parents of adolescents are sometimes taken by surprise when they find these years somewhat lonelier and more isolated than those that came before. Parents need to work harder to create situations in which they can discuss their problems and concerns with others going through similar trials.

The sense of being pushed away can contribute to parents' unease during their own mid-life experience. Well before the children actually leave home, they are becoming more and more independent. Parents may begin to feel unneeded and unwanted. The loss of intimacy and closeness with their children forces parents at times to assess their own activities and future plans in new ways. Children will not continue to be a gateway to new activities and organizations, and they will not continue to be a constant source of intimacy and closeness in family life. Parents need to think about how they will meet these important human needs in their "life after children."

Painful though this process may be, both mothers and fathers need to recognize that it is necessary and important to their own futures as well as to the futures of their children. If they are to be competent and effective as adults, youngsters need to experience the growing independence of the teenage years within the safe limits of home. And parents need to recognize that, although parenting is a wonderful and significant part of their lives, it is not all there is to being an adult. The emotional demands of parenting and the paid and unpaid work it entails change in nature throughout the children's lives. As children grow up, leave home, and eventually form their own families, parents need to think about other work and activities. Their children's teenage years are thus an important developmental phase for parents too.

AFTERWORD

Choices are inherently difficult to make, and this is essentially a book about choices. It is about men and women who have made the decision to commit a good portion of their lives to raising children. We have discussed the ramifications of this decision on the lives of adults, the fact that parenting is hard work and that it limits and shapes what mothers and fathers can do in other spheres, in paid jobs and other social involvements. But the fact that parenting is difficult and time-consuming does not mean that it is work without joy, without substantial satisfactions and rewards. One mother we spoke with talked about the singular pleasure being a parent has brought her. "What I feel for my child is a totally unique kind of love. It's not something that I've felt for any other human being. To have experienced that seems to me to be an important event in my life. For me, having a child is a totally unique expression of love. And one that I'm very, very glad that I've had the chance to experience." Another woman, when asked how she thought her life would be different if she had not had a child, responded, "I

suppose it would be a more selfish life. I don't necessarily mean that in a negative way. But I think we'd
be doing more traveling, more going to the theater and
that type of stuff. I think, though, that life would be
less full. Because being a parent is participating in
things that have happened in Western culture between people for generations. I would have felt
cheated if I hadn't had the opportunity to have a child.
And see him grow. It's been very, very interesting; and
having him love me—I mean, I really like that."

Despite the advantages of parenting, however, it is
helpful for adults to recognize the problems and constraints that define each stage of raising children. Indeed, each new development in a child's life raises
new issues for parents, new questions and new problems to solve. As another parent reflected, "I was
saying to someone the other day that you just get used
to him and the next day he's a different person. It
blows my mind. There's no one else I know like that.
All my adult relationships are fairly constant, but my
child is always changing."

It is unfortunately all too easy for parents to focus on
the problems, difficulties, and hard choices they face at
each stage in their children's lives. Parents need to
remember—and help each other remember—the joy,
creativity, intimacy, and pleasure that youngsters bring
into our lives. In fact, it is often difficult for parents
even to understand the dilemma of the economists we
mentioned earlier who have had such trouble developing a rationale for why people have children. One
parent described a game she plays with her two-year-
old daughter. "If someone came up to me and said,
'What a cute little girl! I'll give you a million, trillion,

zillion dollars for her,' what would I say? I'd say, 'You're not even close,' " she jokes. Her daughter answers, "That's right," laughing into her mother's face, "You'd say, 'Go away, you're not even close.' " "That's right," says the mother. "I'd say 'Go away.' Not all the money in the world could buy my little girl from me." Both mother and daughter then collapse into giggles.

It is the intimacy and closeness, the prospect of watching children grow and develop, that binds us to our sons and daughters, from infancy through adolescence. "I enjoy that I have this super baby," one mother said about her year-old daughter. "She's a great baby, and when I realize that she's so wonderful and that I like her and that we're enjoying each other, it makes me feel kind of proud. I like being connected to that kid. I like the closeness. With my daughter, I love to put my arms around her and I love to kiss her. To have that closeness with her, nursing her, that whole nurturing. I love to hold that little kid in my arms." Another parent talked about his pride in his older son. "I guess we're proud that he seems so talented in several areas, and so happy and bright and athletic. He is a pain in the neck lots of time, and I know he's selfish and not a good sport and all that. But he is a really interesting child to me."

Children even before their birth can inspire parents with a depth of feeling that is unique. Mothers and fathers remember forever the moment when their new baby was put into their arms. "That was the most moving moment of my life," recalls a loving father.

This sense of intimacy and pleasure continues as preschoolers engage their parents in increasingly complex activities. Parents gain satisfaction from their toddler's development. They also learn to respect and enjoy their preschooler's newfound ability to take on the world and to be an interesting and a rewarding companion. One employed mother of a three-year-old daughter fondly recalls an incredibly busy Saturday. "I always worried about the frenetic pace of our lives. Because I was working so hard during the week, even our weekends were just one round of chores after another. I worried that I was simply dragging my little girl from one job to another, always working, always busy, even when I was with her. But one Saturday evening, she turned to me after our busy day—a day we spent shopping, cleaning, cooking, and doing office work together—and she said to me, 'Mommy, we're a team, aren't we? We're a great team.' When I feel pressured and tired, I gain strength myself from my daughter, who saw our work as teamwork rather than as drudgery."

The pride and responsibility parents feel for their children continue through the school years. One father talked about his child, who was having difficulty at school but trying to overcome it. "I'm very proud of the way—it's maybe a funny thing to say—but I'm proud of the way she tries. Sarah is a plugger, she tries with everything. Maybe even excessively. Cooking, sewing—menial things, possibly, to you and to anybody else, but she does the best she can, and she puts all her effort into it." As children progress through school, parents recognize the effort being put into learning and growing, into becoming effective and responsible individuals in their own right.

And then, in adolescence, parents can actually see

the image of the adult their child is becoming. Despite the acknowledged trials of the teenage years, parents are also gratified by seeing their youngsters make their own choices and decisions by experimenting with different values, different ways of acting, and different ways of life. "I admire the authority with which my son speaks," said one mother. "He has his own thoughts now, his own opinions. He can tell what's right and wrong."

The maturation and increasing independence of children is not just a loss. It is also the opportunity to witness the potential of the next generation, to observe its particular strengths as well as its difficulties. As children change, so do their parents and their parents' lives. Having a child keeps adults attuned to the flow of their own lives. On a daily basis, they see how their own lives are played out in the context of the future generation. Raising children is difficult, challenging, demanding, satisfying, rewarding, and pleasurable. It is a totally unique experience, and one that most men and women continue to want at some point in their lives.

SUGGESTED READING

MOTHERS, FATHERS, AND FAMILIES

Bane, Mary Jo. *Here to Stay: American Families in the Twentieth Century*. Basic Books, 1976.

Baruch, Grace; Barnett, Rosalind; Rivers, Caryl. *Lifeprints: New Patterns of Love and Work for Today's Woman*. McGraw-Hill Book Co., 1983.

Daniels, Pamela, and Weingarten, Kathy. *Sooner or Later: The Timing of Parenthood in Adult Lives*. W. W. Norton & Co., 1982.

Fraiberg, Selma. *Every Child's Birthright: In Defense of Mothering*. Basic Books, 1977.

Friedland, Ronnie, and Kort, Carol (eds.). *The Mothers' Book: Shared Experience*. Houghton Mifflin Co., 1981.

Green, Maureen. *Fathering*. McGraw-Hill Book Co., 1976.

Howard, Jane. *Families*. Simon & Schuster, 1978.

Kamerman, Sheila B. *Parenting in an Unresponsive Society: Managing Work and Family Life*. The Free Press, 1980.

Lasch, Christopher. *Haven in a Heartless World: The Family Besieged*. Basic Books, 1977.

Lazarre, Jane. *The Mother Knot*. McGraw-Hill Book Co., 1976.

Lein, Laura. *Families Without Villains*. Lexington Book Co., 1984.

Levine, James. *Who Will Raise the Children?* J. B. Lippincott Co., 1976.

McBride, Angela B. *The Growth and Development of Mothers*. Harper & Row, 1973.

O'Donnell, Lydia. *The Unheralded Majority: Contemporary Women as Mothers*. Lexington Book Co., forthcoming.

Pleck, Joseph H., and Sawyer, Jack (eds.). *Men and Masculinity*. Prentice-Hall, 1974.

Rich, Adrienne. *Of Woman Born*. W. W. Norton & Co., 1976.

Whelan, Elizabeth. *A Baby . . . Maybe: A Guide to Making the Most Fateful Decision of Your Life*. Bobbs-Merrill Co., 1975.

CHILD REARING

Brazelton, T. Berry. *Doctor and Child*. Delacorte Press, 1976.

_____ . *Infants and Parents*. Delacorte Press, 1969.

_____ . *Toddlers and Parents*. Delacorte Press, 1974.

Church, Joseph. *Understanding Your Child from Birth to Three*. Random House, 1973.

Fraiberg, Selma. *The Magic Years*. Charles Scribner's Sons, 1959.

Newson, John, and Newson, Elizabeth. *Toys and Playthings: In Development and Remediation*. Pantheon Books, 1975.

Parents' Choice: A Review of Children's Media. For subscription information, write P.O. Box 185, Waban, Mass. 02168.

Pogrebin, Letty C. *Growing Up Free: Raising Your Child in the 80's*. McGraw-Hill Book Co., 1980.

Singer, Dorothy G., and Singer, J. L. *Partners in Play*. Harper & Row, 1977.

Spock, Benjamin. *Raising Children in a Difficult Time*. Pocket Books, 1976.

WOMEN'S AND MEN'S ADULT DEVELOPMENT

Friedan, Betty. *The Second Stage*. Summit Books, 1981.

Gilligan, Carol. *In a Different Voice: Psychological Theory and Women's Development.* Harvard University Press, 1982.

Miller, Jean Baker. *Toward a New Psychology of Women.* Beacon Press, 1976.

Sheehy, Gail. *Pathfinders.* William Morrow & Co., 1981.